THE DEPARTMENT OF HOMELAND SECURITY'S FIRST YEAR

These materials are a product of The Century Foundation's Homeland Security Project, which is supported by the John D. and Catherine T. MacArthur Foundation, the John S. and James L. Knight Foundation, the Robert Wood Johnson Foundation, and the Carnegie Corporation of New York. To help formulate sound ideas for strengthening the nation's homeland security in ways that will receive broad public support, this project organized bipartisan, expert working groups focusing on the federal response, federalism issues, the public's need to know, bioterrorism, and immigration. Their mission is to provide policy recommendations and oversee the production of explanatory issue briefs and longer publications to help inform the nation's continuing search for answers in this complex and sensitive area of public policy. More details about the membership of these groups and the publications produced in connection with the project are available at www.tcf.org and www.homelandsec.org.

THE DEPARTMENT OF HOMELAND SECURITY'S FIRST YEAR

A REPORT CARD

Donald F. Kettl, editor

A CENTURY FOUNDATION REPORT

THE CENTURY FOUNDATION PRESS ◆ NEW YORK

The Century Foundation sponsors and supervises timely analyses of economic policy, foreign affairs, and domestic political issues. Not-for-profit and nonpartisan, it was founded in 1919 and endowed by Edward A. Filene.

LIBRARY OF CONGRESS CATALOGING-IN-PUBLICATION DATA

The Department of Homeland Security's first year : a report card.
   p. cm.
 Edited by Donald F. Kettl.
 "A Century Foundation report."
 Includes bibliographical references (p.   ).
 ISBN 0-87078-486-2 (pbk. : alk. paper)
 1. United States. Dept. of Homeland Security. 2. Terrorism—United States—Prevention. I. Kettl, Donald F.
 HV6432.4.D46 2004
 353.3'0973—dc22

                                                                    2004005770

CONTENTS

Overview
Donald F. Kettl   1

1. Aviation Security
    E. Marla Felcher   29

2. Intelligence Gathering, Analysis, and Sharing
    Gregory F. Treverton   55

3. Immigration
    T. Alexander Aleinikoff   77

4. Strengthening State and Local Terrorism
    Prevention and Response
    Anne M. Khademian   97

    Notes   119

    Index   141

    About the Contributors   151

OVERVIEW

Donald F. Kettl

When George W. Bush proposed the creation of the Department of Homeland Security (DHS) on June 8, 2002, he called it "the most extensive reorganization of the federal government since the 1940s."[1] Indeed, at its inception on March 1, 2003, the DHS brought together twenty-two federal agencies and more than 170,000 employees—the largest restructuring since the creation of the Department of Defense (DOD) in 1947 (for an organizational chart of the DHS, see Appendix, page 25). Although the DOD reorganization involved more employees, by almost any other measure the DHS restructuring was harder.

Even the large numbers vastly understate the scale and complexity of the job. As with past reorganizations, all the agencies involved were still responsible for carrying out their previous mandates—from the Coast Guard's rescue of sailors in distress to the Federal Emergency Management Agency's relief for victims of natural disasters. But unlike what happened in previous reorganizations, all of the agencies took on new and expanded homeland security responsibilities. Thus, the scale and complexity of the job make this the most challenging reorganization ever attempted in America.

Now that the new department has been in operation for a year, how has it performed?

The Century Foundation commissioned prominent experts to undertake detailed studies, which are presented in the chapters that follow, focused on four critical homeland security challenges: aviation security, intelligence gathering and coordination, immigration, and coordination with state and local governments. The grades presented here derive directly from those reports, focusing on the core elements of the department's mission arising from the gaping security vulnerabilities so tragically illuminated on September 11, 2001:

- *Aviation security.* Federal officials were concerned with more than the fact that terrorists breached airport security on September 11 to hijack the planes. Subsequent investigation revealed vulnerabilities not only in the screening of passengers but also of carry-on and checked luggage. Reformers called on the new department to enhance aviation security.

- *Intelligence gathering and coordination.* In the months that followed September 11, analysts and reporters alike constantly asked how the government's intelligence community failed to detect and prevent the attacks. When it became clear that bits and pieces of intelligence had been collected but had never been linked, reformers called for an aggressive effort to do better at "connecting the dots" among the nation's intelligence agencies. They called on the new department to play a strong role in that effort.

- *Immigration.* Federal investigators were stunned to discover that the September 11 hijackers appeared to have entered the country legally, although staff members of the independent National Commission on Terrorist Attacks Upon the United States believe that at least two, and perhaps eight, of the hijackers had used fraudulent visas. Reformers, both within and outside of the government, have called on the new department to improve the enforcement of immigration laws and to tighten security at the nation's borders.

- *Coordination with state and local governments.* The heroic efforts of the "first responders"—local police, firefighters, paramedics, and other emergency workers—on the morning of September 11 demonstrated how crucial state and local governments were in the war against terrorism. Follow-up studies revealed that many of the nation's state and local governments were not nearly as well prepared as the first responders in New York and Washington. Reformers called on the new department to improve coordination of federal strategies with state and local governments.

Based on those studies, this report card also assesses the overall management performance of the DHS leadership during its first year.

GRADING THE DEPARTMENT OF HOMELAND SECURITY

So how does the department's performance measure up after a year? This report card is based on:

- **Strategy.** How well has the DHS focused the nation's energy on improving its security?

- **Capacity.** How well has the DHS strengthened the federal government's ability to meet the goals of this strategy?

- **Results.** How has the DHS actually improved homeland security?

The report card applies these criteria to the four policy areas and to the department's management performance. The grading scale:

> A – excellent: could not be significantly improved
> B – above average: needs some work
> C – average: needs considerable improvement
> D – poor: backsliding from earlier conditions

After its first year, what grades has the new Department of Homeland Security earned?

DEPARTMENT OF HOMELAND SECURITY — FIRST YEAR	
OVERALL GRADE	**C+**
Aviation Security	B–
Intelligence	B–
Immigration	B–
Coordination with State and Local Governments	C
DHS Management	C+

DETAILED DEPARTMENT OF HOMELAND SECURITY REPORT CARD

OVERALL GRADE	C+
AVIATION SECURITY	**B–**
◆ Hire checkpoint screeners	A
◆ Conduct timely screener background checks	D
◆ Create adequate system for ongoing background checks of screeners	A
◆ Train screeners	B
◆ Measure screener performance	C
◆ Screen checked luggage	B
◆ Put undercover federal air marshals on flights	A
◆ Oversee contractors	B
◆ Create passenger profiles	C
◆ Control access to airport perimeters	C
◆ Control access to secure airport areas	C
◆ Ensure security in general aviation (private planes)	D
◆ Ensure security in air cargo	D
◆ Coordinate air security with foreign governments	B
INTELLIGENCE	**B–**
◆ Get DHS Information Analysis and Infrastructure Protection Directorate up and running	A
◆ Integrate DHS intelligence into Terrorist Threat Integration Center	B
◆ Create clear mission and strategy for analysis of information about possible attacks	C
◆ Coordinate DHS threat assessment with infrastructure protection	B–
◆ Share information with state and local officials	C

DETAILED DEPARTMENT OF HOMELAND SECURITY REPORT CARD (Cont'd.)

IMMIGRATION	**B–**
ENFORCEMENT	**B–**
◆ Combine immigration, customs, and agriculture functions into a single point of enforcement at the border	B
◆ Strengthen entry and exit controls at ports of entry	B
◆ Strengthen entry and exit controls at land borders	C
◆ Develop, in coordination with other nations, machine-readable biometric passports for foreign visitors	C
◆ Track entry and matriculation of foreign students	A
◆ Protect critical infrastructure	B
◆ Prevent illegal entry at the border	C–
◆ Develop a unified cadre of interior enforcement agents	B
◆ Undertake targeted enforcement efforts inside the country (to reduce smuggling, for example)	B
◆ Apprehend those who overstay visas	C
IMMIGRATION AND NATURALIZATION SERVICES	**C+**
◆ Improve customer service at local immigration offices	B–
◆ Reduce backlog of immigration and naturalization cases	D
COMBINED FUNCTIONS	**B–**
◆ Integrate immigration databases	B
◆ Integrate policy development	C

Continued

DETAILED DEPARTMENT OF HOMELAND SECURITY REPORT CARD (Cont'd.)

COORDINATION WITH STATE AND LOCAL GOVERNMENTS	**C**
◆ Develop a national strategy for homeland security	C
◆ Get DHS Office of State and Local Government Coordination up and running	B
◆ Allocate money based on the risk of a terrorist attack	D
◆ Establish lines of communication with state governments	B
◆ Get money out the door to state governments	C
◆ Consolidate training, equipment, and planning grants for the states	C
◆ Improve overall accessibility and flexibility of grant money to local governments and first responders	D
◆ Provide training for local first responders	C
◆ Define expectations for states and local governments as partners in homeland security	C
DHS MANAGEMENT	**C+**
◆ Create clear and measurable goals for assessing performance	C
◆ Implement the new DHS personnel system	C
◆ Manage relationships with foreign counterparts	B
◆ Establish a clearer and more useful national warning system	B
◆ Integrate disparate agencies into a coordinated department	C
◆ Provide strong leadership on homeland security	B
◆ Work with Congress and other key interests to develop clear policy goals	D

The DHS's overall grade for its first year is C+. As is scarcely surprising given the enormity of the task it faced, the department's performance has varied widely. In some areas, the DHS has done exceptionally well, yet in other areas, conditions are worse than before the DHS was created. The biggest areas needing improvement, in fact, deal with the very coordination—"connecting the dots"— problems that the department was created to solve.

How much progress can be ascribed to the creation of the department itself? Its advocates originally contended that putting the homeland security function into a department would give the new secretary more clout in pulling the disparate functions together and would give homeland security more leverage in the budgetary process. However, there is not yet much evidence that the department has met these aspirations. The higher grades mainly apply to ongoing functions, where the DHS built progress on preexisting momentum. (One notable exception is the restructuring of the Immigration and Naturalization Service [INS], which improved integration of enforcement efforts.) On the other hand, the lower grades go mainly to the very coordination problems the department was created to solve. Especially when it comes to directing aid strategically to state and local governments, there is little evidence that the creation of the department has improved coordinating clout or budgetary focus.

More details about the grades and supporting analysis are included in the individual reports; this summary details the areas with highest and lowest performance.

AREAS WITH HIGH PERFORMANCE

The Department of Homeland Security has done well in these five areas:

- *Tracking the entry and matriculation of foreign students.* Some of the September 11 hijackers were in the country on student visas. Although there has been considerable complaint from students and universities, the DHS has improved its ability to track foreign students and their activities.

- *Hiring checkpoint screeners.* The DHS faced the massive job of moving the Transportation Security Administration (TSA) from the Department of Transportation, hiring a huge federal work-force, and integrating the screeners into a solid system. The system has emerged far more quickly—and functioned far better—than almost anyone expected.

- *Creating an effective ongoing system for conducting screener background checks.* After a rocky start, in which screeners were allowed to remain on duty even after officials determined they had serious criminal records, the department has made huge strides in ensuring that screeners meet security standards.

- *Expanding federal air marshal coverage on planes.* In one year, the Transportation Security Administration expanded the undercover air marshal service from thirty-three to more than four thousand agents. The DHS subsequently expanded the program to include eleven thousand agents by creating a corps of "reserve" marshals who are sent to planes only when the DHS perceives an increased threat to aviation security.

- *Getting the DHS Information Analysis and Infrastructure Protection Directorate up and running.* Congress charged the new department with collecting and integrating information about critical infrastructure—bridges, roads, tunnels, airports, and highways—that might be vulnerable to attack. In short order, the DHS has launched the directorate charged with this responsibility.

AREAS WITH SERIOUS PERFORMANCE PROBLEMS

In these six areas, however, the department has shown serious short-comings:

- *Ensuring security in general aviation (private planes).* Although the DHS has substantially improved security for travelers on the airlines, security remains loose for private planes and some small airports. This increases the chances that terrorists could use private planes to launch attacks.

- *Ensuring security in air cargo.* Although federal screeners examine baggage checked onto commercial airliners, there is no similar system for freight carried on the nation's—indeed, the world's—massive air cargo system. The Transportation Security Administration estimates there is a 35 percent to 65 percent chance that terrorists are planning to place a bomb in the cargo of a U.S. passenger plane. Yet, only about 5 percent of air cargo is screened, even if it is transported on passenger planes. The cargo companies have worked with the DHS to strengthen security, but the system remains vulnerable.

- *Reducing the backlog of immigration and naturalization cases.* In the aftermath of the September 11 attacks, everyone agreed that the nation had to do a far better job of processing immigration and naturalization cases. Because of the pressures of integrating these operations into the new department, delays in security checks, and an agency culture that would rather say no than yes to avoid any chance of admitting a terrorist, the problem is now worse than it was when the department was created. Of all the goals set with the launch of the DHS, the department's performance most often has fallen short here.

- *Allocating federal grant money to state and local governments based on the risk of an attack.* The promised federal aid to state and local governments has flowed slowly. Money already distributed has been allocated more on the basis of pork than need. Because of the enormous political issues involved, including decisions by Congress, money may be sent where it is less needed, leaving areas at highest risk underfunded. The DHS must devise a system to help link money to risk.

- *Using federal grant funds to strengthen state and local government first responders.* Of the money that has gone to state and local governments, relatively little has found its way to first responders. State and local governments, already severely pinched by the worst budget crisis in half a century, have struggled to strengthen their capability to respond to terrorist attacks. The DHS must work with administration officials to fashion a budget that puts money where it is needed.

- *Working with Congress and key stakeholders, including representatives of the nation's state and local governments and key officials in other government agencies, to develop clear policy goals.* While widespread debate continues about how to strengthen homeland security, the nation is far from reaching a consensus on what this means, and the DHS has yet to articulate a clear vision. But the difficulty here also lies with Congress and the crosscutting political pressures surrounding the issue. Performance has been poor, but the fault is not entirely that of the DHS.

AVIATION SECURITY GRADE: B–

The repeated images of hijacked planes crashing into the World Trade Center made aviation security the biggest symbol of the nation's new war on terrorism. It was more than a matter of protection, to prevent another similar attack. It was a matter for the nation's economy, to keep the attacks from crippling the critical transportation industry. And it was a matter for the nation's psychic health, to reduce the sense of vulnerability.

Thus, one of the new department's first tasks was strengthening aviation security to prevent a repeat of the September 11 attacks and to encourage a nervous public to return to the skies. In many respects, the DHS performed well in solving some extraordinarily complex problems.

SCREENERS. The TSA faced a daunting challenge: hiring and training 55,600 airport screeners in just thirteen months. The effort was well under way before the restructuring moved the TSA into the new DHS, but it nevertheless became one of the big tasks department officials faced.

The TSA quickly recruited that workforce. However, almost two thousand of the screeners had to be fired because they had criminal records, including manslaughter, rape, and burglary. The department's own inspector general found that some screeners stayed on the payroll and kept their badges as the TSA worked through the cumbersome process of firing them. In some cases, that took weeks or months.

Most of the problems came from cursory reviews by the TSA's contractors and from lax TSA oversight of those contractors. In some cases, screeners were allowed to begin work before their background checks were completed. In other cases, the contractors left five hundred boxes of forms and background information unprocessed for months.[2] The DHS has fired the contractors responsible and has taken steps to vet screeners more quickly and thoroughly.

FEDERAL AIR MARSHALS. The TSA likewise has vastly increased the number of undercover air marshals from just thirty-three on September 11, 2001, to between four thousand and six thousand today. (The exact number of marshals and which flights they are on are both closely guarded secrets.) The air marshals have had a dual effect: improving security on commercial airplanes and reassuring the flying public.

But progress in other areas of aviation security has been far slower.

GENERAL AVIATION (PRIVATE PLANES). The vast majority of private planes can still fly where they want, when they want. During the orange alert in late 2003, a small plane entered the controlled airspace around LaGuardia Airport, flew down the East River, and circled the Statue of Liberty before an armed police helicopter escorted it to an airport on Long Island. The TSA said that "measures taken by individual operators are more comprehensive than regulations at the state or federal level," but the measures are voluntary, and it is unclear which measures have been instituted and by whom. The lack of security for general aviation contrasts sharply with the high security for commercial airlines.

AIR CARGO. Last year, more than 12 million tons of cargo and mail were transported by air in the United States. About 75 percent of air cargo is shipped on cargo-only planes. The rest, about 3 million tons annually, flies on commercial flights, in the holds of planes along with passengers' suitcases.[3] The Transportation Security Administration estimates there is a 35 percent to 65 percent chance that terrorists are planning to place a bomb in the cargo of a U.S. passenger plane. Yet, only about 5 percent of air cargo is screened, even if it is transported on passenger planes.[4] The U.S. General Accounting Office in November 2003 reported that cargo carried aboard cargo-only as well as on commercial passenger flights continues to be highly vulnerable to terrorists' bombs.[5]

RECOMMENDATIONS

Both the air cargo and general aviation industries agree that it is impossible to improve security without hurting their businesses. This is the same complaint, of course, that the commercial airlines made to Congress and the Federal Aviation Administration before the terrorist attacks of September 11—that stepped-up passenger and baggage screening would slow down their operations, scare away customers, and lead to the death of an industry that was vital to the American economy. Yet, after the attacks, Congress found a way to improve security and keep people flying. A similarly aggressive effort is needed in air cargo and general aviation. The case of the man who, late in 2003, shipped himself in an air cargo container from New York to Dallas illustrates how vulnerable the system is.

History has demonstrated that, in the absence of a terrorist attack, neither the air cargo nor general aviation industries will voluntarily take the steps needed to secure their fleets adequately. Stowaways on board cargo planes have recently drawn attention to the system's vulnerabilities. Therefore, Congress and the DHS must use their authority to impose new standards. The following steps would be a good start:

- mandatory background checks for all general aviation pilots;

- mandatory airport security screening, similar to the screening currently imposed on commercial airline passengers, for all general aviation and air cargo pilots and passengers;

- mandatory measures to secure general aviation planes at airports, such as airport surveillance cameras and aircraft and hangar locks to prevent theft;

- mandatory screening of all air cargo carried on commercial passenger planes; and

- significant investment by the DHS in research and development of cargo screening technology.

INTELLIGENCE GRADE: B–

An irony lies at the core of the Department of Homeland Security's work on intelligence: when Congress brought together twenty-two different agencies involved in homeland security, it left out the federal government's intelligence operations. The strongest argument for creating the department—to improve the government's ability to coordinate and integrate information available to different agencies—proved to be the one big issue that restructuring did not even attempt to solve.

From the first days after the September 11 attacks, the driving goal of those proposing a new department was the need to "connect the dots"—to strengthen linkages among the government agencies charged with collecting and analyzing data. The explosive testimony of Coleen Rowley, chief counsel of the FBI's Minneapolis field office, made the new department's creation inevitable. In June 2002, Rowley told the Senate Judiciary Committee that top FBI officials did not act on warnings that suspicious individuals were receiving flight training. That same evening, President Bush appeared on national television. After fighting the creation of a new department, he switched his position and urged Congress to create the Department of Homeland Security.

Neither the Bush proposal nor the leading congressional alternatives envisioned uniting the government's far-flung intelligence empire—the CIA, the FBI, the National Security Agency, as well as the intelligence operations of the departments of Defense and State—into the new department. All of these agencies retained their independence. Instead of giving the DHS the responsibility for connecting the dots of threats to the homeland, the administration created a new Terrorist Threat Integration Center (TTIC) designed to improve the sharing of information but reporting to the head of the CIA.

Simply getting the new TTIC operation up and running proved no mean feat. Indeed, the TTIC became a new arena in which the FBI and the CIA continued their ongoing scuffles over domestic and foreign intelligence. The irresistible campaign for establishing the DHS grew from the debate about coordinating intelligence, but after its creation, the DHS largely found itself at the periphery of these issues. The TTIC has demonstrated progress in coordinating intelligence, but, as the federal government's primary user of homeland security intelligence, the DHS's marginal role in the collection and analysis process has hindered its ability to lead homeland security policy.

It was the "connect the dots" problem on intelligence that provided the strongest push for creating the department. But the new department has been only one player—the junior partner, at that—in intelligence issues. Indeed, despite the arguments about the need to connect the dots, intelligence coordination remains one of the largest and most important unresolved issues in homeland security. There are several steps that the DHS should take in attacking these issues.

RECOMMENDATIONS

◆ *Clarify the DHS relationship with the TTIC.* Serious problems of overlapping responsibility continue within the TTIC. While the nation's intelligence agencies should continue to work to strengthen the TTIC, the DHS must clarify its own role in the TTIC—and its working relationships with the other federal agencies responsible for collecting and analyzing intelligence.

◆ *Clarify the DHS intelligence role.* Through the work of Transportation Security Administration screeners, border patrol officials, and other department officials, the DHS can collect a great deal of useful information, and this information should be made an integral part of the nation's intelligence assets. Once Congress and the president more clearly define the DHS intelligence priorities, the department must link intelligence information more effectively to the job of protecting the nation's critical infrastructure.

◆ *Develop a clear protocol for sharing intelligence information with state and local officials.* Officials in state and local governments repeatedly have complained that federal officials share little useful intelligence information. Indeed, some officials have said they rely more on CNN than on the DHS, the FBI, and the CIA. There are valid concerns about ensuring the security of intelligence information, but the DHS should take the lead in establishing clear procedures for providing state and local officials with better information to help guide their own homeland security decisions.

- *Clarify standards for collecting and retaining data.* Through a wide variety of databases, the DHS and the TTIC are collecting substantial volumes of information about Americans. Congress, the Bush administration, and the courts need to provide clear guidance about what information can—and should—be collected, how it should be safeguarded, and how long this information should be retained.

IMMIGRATION GRADE: B–

Federal officials have been discussing immigration reform for many years. The Immigration and Naturalization Service has long been known as one of the government's most troubled agencies, both under-resourced and undermanaged. Millions of applicants wait for their applications to be resolved; millions of undocumented migrants reside within the United States with little likelihood of being apprehended.

The debate churned with little action—until the September 11 attacks pushed it to center stage. All nineteen of the hijackers were non-citizens. Most had entered the United States legally, although it is possible that some had cleverly forged passports. At the time of the attacks, most were legally residing in the country. Some of the hijackers entered on student visas, but they were no longer attending classes. Some were in the country illegally. And the information systems failed to connect the dots with the intelligence collected elsewhere in the government.

Months after they flew planes into the World Trade Center towers, immigration documents for two of the hijackers arrived at a Venice, Florida, flight school. The story stunned many officials, including President Bush, who called it inexcusable. The incident was misreported—the paperwork turned out to be copies of visas approved in July and August 2001. But the specter of a system where the paper flow was so badly out of sync with reality turned up the heat on the immigration system and further fueled the movement toward reform.

Reform of the immigration system—keeping people out of the country who might be a threat and ensuring that visitors do not over-stay their visas—became a top priority.

In some areas, the Department of Homeland Security has made significant progress.

TRACKING THE ENTRY AND MATRICULATION OF FOREIGN STUDENTS. Efforts to improve the student tracking system have been long in the works, although the response to the September 11 attacks accelerated the process. The information system for tracking foreign students at American colleges, universities, and other educational institutions has vastly improved. There have been considerable complaints from both students and the institutions, in part because of privacy fears, in part because of fears that implementation of the policy promoted racism, and in part because of the high cost. Nevertheless, the new system has strengthened the department's ability to track foreign students and their activities.

However, in other areas, the DHS not only has failed to make progress; it has lost ground.

REDUCING THE BACKLOG OF IMMIGRATION AND NATURALIZATION CASES. Visitors seeking green cards, work authorization, and naturalization have swamped immigration officials. Even the department's staunchest defenders agree that the DHS has to do a far better job. But the situation has gotten worse. In March 2003, the department's Citizenship and Information Services (USCIS) faced a backlog of 5.2 million immigration applications that had to be processed and resolved. At the end of October 2003, the number was more than 5.4 million. The number of pending naturalization applications remained virtually unchanged at more than six hundred thousand, even though the number of filings fell by 25 percent in fiscal year 2003.

RECOMMENDATIONS

- ◆ *Fix the immigration system.* In large part, this is a matter of resources; it is also a matter of management. Long delays are unfair to those who have a right to legal status and to their families, employers, and communities. The DHS is far away from achieving the administration's goal of reducing the backlog.

◆ ***Strengthen controls at the nation's land borders.*** One of the
biggest problems in safeguarding the nation's borders has long
been simply tracking who enters and leaves—and which short-
term visitors have overstayed their visas. The DHS has made
progress in integrating the nation's immigration, customs, and
security operations at the borders. But more progress needs to
be made. New procedures for capturing biometric identifiers—
fingerprints and photos electronically stored on the government's computer system—apply only to a small percentage of
noncitizens identified as high risk who enter the United States.
Furthermore, no significant new steps have been taken to prevent
or deter the flow of hundreds of thousands of undocumented
immigrants across U.S. borders. The DHS also needs to strengthen
further the integration of these operations—and their connection to the databases that identify possible terrorists. The new
Terrorist Screening Center is an important step toward the goal
of linking the dozen watch lists kept by the nine different agencies that now track suspects.[6]

COORDINATION WITH STATE AND LOCAL GOVERNMENTS GRADE: C

The nation's response to the September 11 attacks is enshrined in the
heroic tales of the first responders—local police, firefighters, paramedics, and other emergency workers—in New York and Washington
who risked and, in hundreds of cases, sacrificed their lives to save
thousands of people. The attacks drove home the importance to the
nation of having a strong local first response. If terrorism can present
a threat anytime and anywhere, the nation needs its state and local
governments to create a well-integrated system of response.

Congress charged the new department with collecting and integrating information about critical infrastructure—bridges, roads, tunnels,
airports, and highways—that might be vulnerable to attack. In short
order, the DHS has launched the Information Analysis and Infrastructure
Protection Directorate, which is charged with this set of challenges.

But key federal promises to improve coordination with state and
local governments have gone unmet. As a task force of the Markle

Foundation put it: "DHS has yet to articulate a vision of how it will link federal, state, and local agencies in a communications and sharing network, or what its role will be with respect to the TTIC and other federal agencies."[7]

FEDERAL AID TO STATE AND LOCAL GOVERNMENTS. In the aftermath of the September 11 attacks, the federal government promised substantial aid to state and local governments to help support their first responders. However, the promised federal grants have been slow in flowing—and the money has been distributed more on the basis of pork than on the basis of need. In 2003, for example, the state of Wyoming received $35 per capita, compared with New York and California, which received about $5 per person.[8] Because of the enormous political pressures in Congress, the nation risks sending money where it is less needed. And it risks underfunding areas that are most vulnerable to attack.

AIDING FIRST RESPONDERS. Of the money that has gone to state and local governments, relatively little has found its way to first responders—in part because of cumbersome DHS procedures in getting the money out. The recent Gilmore Commission (Advisory Panel to Assess Domestic Response Capabilities for Terrorism Involving Weapons of Mass Destruction) report found that 71 percent of law enforcement organizations and more than half of paid and volunteer fire departments reported no increases in funding, including from the federal government, following September 11, 2001.[9] State and local governments, already severely pinched by the worst budget crisis in half a century, have struggled to strengthen their capacity to respond to terrorist attacks.

RECOMMENDATIONS

◆   *Allocate scarce federal money to where it is most needed.* Allowing federal homeland security grants to degenerate into pork-barrel politics would damage homeland security in two ways. It would waste scarce budget dollars in places where the money is needed less. And it would undermine the always uneasy political support for homeland security programs. The department has launched a quiet but important initiative to assess risk as a way to channel resources to where the money is needed most. That program ought to be put into overdrive.

* **Strengthen the coordination of state and local governments.** It is one thing to strengthen first responders. That is the cornerstone of the state and local homeland security effort. But that is not enough. Any serious terrorist attack will quickly overwhelm even the largest first-response systems, and it will overrun the systems of most small- and medium-sized communities. The federal and state governments need to focus far more on encouraging collaboration among local governments, especially in systems for communication among neighboring communities, mutual-aid agreements, and effective strategies for dealing with chemical and biological threats. The spring 2003 Top Officials exercise (TOPOFF), which simulated an attack using a dirty bomb in Seattle and the pneumonic plague in Chicago, tested the ability of federal, state, and local officials to coordinate their responses. The test revealed deep problems, including flaws in communication and uncertainty about who was responsible for what.[10]

* **Devise a strategy for best making use of the Directorate for Emergency Preparedness (DEP; formerly the Federal Emergency Management Agency) and the Office of Domestic Preparedness.** These two units of the DHS have overlapping responsibilities: the DEP distributes grants for public health, medical preparedness, and disaster response training, while the Office of Domestic Preparedness (ODP) does so for terrorism prevention and response. The DHS needs to make a basic strategic decision between an "all-risk" strategy, which would combine terrorism and natural disaster efforts, and maintaining separate capabilities for those dangers. The all-risk approach would presume that the implications for first responders are nearly identical between terrorist attacks and events like earthquakes and tornadoes. If the DHS followed that course, the work of the DEP and the ODP would need to be far more strongly integrated. On the other hand, settling on the strategy of maintaining distinct capabilities would require strengthening both agencies in pursuit of their separate challenges while improving their coordination. To date, however, the lack of a clear strategy has created confusion—and the risk of inadequate preparation and response.

DHS MANAGEMENT GRADE: C+

The creation of the new Department of Homeland Security has posed a management challenge of stunning—indeed, unprecedented—difficulty.

SCALE. The number of agencies (twenty-two) moved into the new department ranks this effort among the largest reorganizations in American history. The number of employees (more than 170,000) merged into the new department is larger than for any other federal reorganization since the creation of the Department of Defense in 1947. Although the DOD reorganization involved more employees, the DHS restructuring was, in many ways, far more complex.

RISK. Not only is Secretary Tom Ridge charged with managing such an enormous restructuring, but also he must do so at a time of great risk. Any error could increase the nation's vulnerability and increase the potential for a devastating attack. It is very much like trying to rebuild a car as it barrels down the highway at eighty miles per hour.

LOCATION. The restructuring occurred without physically moving the related agencies to the same location. When the Department of Defense was created, the key agencies were already located in the Pentagon. But few of the agencies transferred to the new Department of Homeland Security actually changed locations. The secretary and the department's key staff work out of the headquarters on Nebraska Avenue, but the DHS empire stretches over miles of Washington real estate. One of the arguments for the creation of the new department was to bridge the barriers created by different organizational cultures. The lack of physical proximity has made it more difficult to solve this cultural problem. The fact that most DHS agencies continue to operate in their old locations has continued to reinforce the old, sometimes dysfunctional, cultures.

PERSONNEL. A central battle in creating the new department was establishing a new, more flexible personnel system. The department has made progress, but the big political battles and many of the operating details still must be resolved.

POLITICAL MANAGEMENT. While managing the department's internal operations, Secretary Ridge faces an enormous challenge in managing the department's vast and complex relationships with external political forces. American Enterprise Institute scholar Norman J. Ornstein counted thirteen House and Senate committees with at least some jurisdiction over homeland security, along with more than sixty subcommittees.[11] In addition, the secretary and his senior staff spend a lot of time dealing with threat analysis, coordinating with other federal agencies, and increasingly working with foreign governments. Simply tending to the department's ongoing political relationships with key decisionmakers, coupled with the task of keeping on top of intelligence briefings, requires an enormous amount of senior managers' time.

ADMINISTRATIVE MANAGEMENT. Top officials have been able to devote relatively little time to the vast management problems of getting such a large operation up and running. Most of the department's senior officials are so buried under the pressing day-to-day operational issues that they have little energy and less time to devote to resolving the department's considerable management issues, which means that the issues are not resolved. The longer these issues fester, the worse the problems can become—and the greater the chance that they open the door to terrorists.

The following recommendations are reactions to several imbalances in the department's structure and operations.

RECOMMENDATIONS

The key to strengthening homeland security is devising new and more effective strategies for coordination: efforts to prevent attacks with tactics to enhance response should attacks occur, and efforts to assess threats with tactics to protect critical infrastructure. The primary reason for creating the department was to improve coordination. While there has been some progress on this front, much more needs to be done. In particular:

♦   *Mission and priorities.* Even though the demand for better integration of intelligence prompted the creation of the department, the DHS is a small player in relation to other government agencies engaged in homeland security. The department's purpose started out muddy and remains so, but it must articulate, far more clearly, its priorities. The only way to do its job better is to define better what its job is. Some of the confusion undoubtedly flows from political cross-pressures and, especially, from the conflicting demands of so many congressional overseers. But top departmental officials, led by the secretary, must be clear about what it is the department seeks to do—and what its distinctive contribution to the nation's homeland security will be.

It might be asking too much for a wide-ranging department in its infancy to have clearly defined priorities. But at this point, the department should have a strategy for creating its strategy. If that is ever going to happen, it will have to be a process launched and guided by the secretary.

- *Prevention versus response.* Even though there was universal agreement on the need to strengthen the nation's ability to respond to terrorist attacks, the DHS has invested most of its energy in preventing attacks. This is understandable—even, perhaps, correct, given the risks that the nation faces. But the department shares responsibility for prevention, and it has primary responsibility for improving response. The fiscal year 2005 budget reflects this problem—there is more money for prevention efforts, but grants for state and local first responders are $805 million less than in fiscal year 2004. Given the problems that state and local governments face, as outlined above, this is moving in the wrong direction.

  The DHS must continue to work to help prevent attacks, but it must strengthen its response strategy as well. If it does not help create a coordinated strategy of response—at the federal, state, and local levels—the nation will remain seriously endangered.

- *Management.* Where federal departments have had the most effective internal management, it has been through the deputy secretary. Separate management offices are typically ignored because management problems are woven into the very fabric of federal departments—and because solving them requires muscle from the top. There are numerous examples of deputy secretaries who have reshaped the management of their departments. Mortimer Downey in the Department of Transportation and T. J. Glauthier in the Department of Energy played such roles in the Clinton administration, and the President's Management Council has for a decade provided strong, ongoing support for such work. Secretary Ridge should strengthen the role of the department's deputy secretary in improving the management of the department.

- *Rethink the department's building blocks.* Congress and President Bush created the Department of Homeland Security not just for functional reasons but, perhaps more important, to be seen to be taking action. Deciding what to move into the department—and what to leave out—preoccupied most of the debate. And the debate centered mostly on how the September 11 terrorists exploited holes in the system to launch their devastating attacks.

The great risk of this approach is that the department could find itself, in organizational and perhaps operational terms, focusing on responding to the last attack instead of focusing on how best to prevent the next. It risks concentrating on preventing another September 11–style attack just as terrorists seek new tactics that exploit other holes in the system. Moving organizational boxes is the traditional approach to administrative reorganization, but it risks being a twentieth-century approach to a twenty-first-century problem.

The nation is dealing not just with one terrorist foe but with many, and the terrorists are clever and creative. Any collection of agencies, no matter how structured, will leave some gaps, and the terrorists' goal is to find these gaps. A solution based primarily on reorganization risks solving an old problem only to create new ones. If, in the process, top officials are so preoccupied by terrorist threats that they pay insufficient attention to departmental management, they risk breeding even more terrorist opportunities. Terrorists operate most effectively when they can identify and exploit gaps in the system. If management problems leave large gaps in communication and coordination, that can create critical openings for terrorists.

In management terms, better homeland security depends on enhanced capacity and stronger coordination. To do better on both fronts, the Department of Homeland Security should create an organizational "tiger team" with two goals: (1) to recommend how to improve the department's organizational capacity for homeland security and (2) to explore alternatives, beyond the shifting of agencies, to enhance coordination.

CONCLUSION

Terrorism presents a new, asymmetric, twenty-first-century threat. Government needs to respond with a new, more flexible, information-based and coordination-driven system. Bolstering the department's structure with a "virtual" department linked by information systems could be one alternative. Much of homeland security—both prevention and response—relies on coordination, and much of the coordination hinges on information. Stronger information systems could make homeland security more flexible and, in turn, build more powerful partnerships among federal, state, and local governments.

The key is to devise a governmental strategy for homeland security that matches the nature of the threat. Terrorism is, by its nature, unpredictable. To be effective, government must be light on its feet. Its organizational structure can limit its vision and hinder its response. If its structure for homeland security is in turbulence, the problems multiply. Government needs new resources, like improved computer systems and better protective gear for first responders. It also needs to be engaged in the management imperatives that will enable the system to be just as lithe, creative, and flexible as the threat it faces.

APPENDIX

ORGANIZATION OF THE
DEPARTMENT OF HOMELAND SECURITY

APPENDIX

ORGANIZATION OF THE DEPARTMENT OF HOMELAND SECURITY

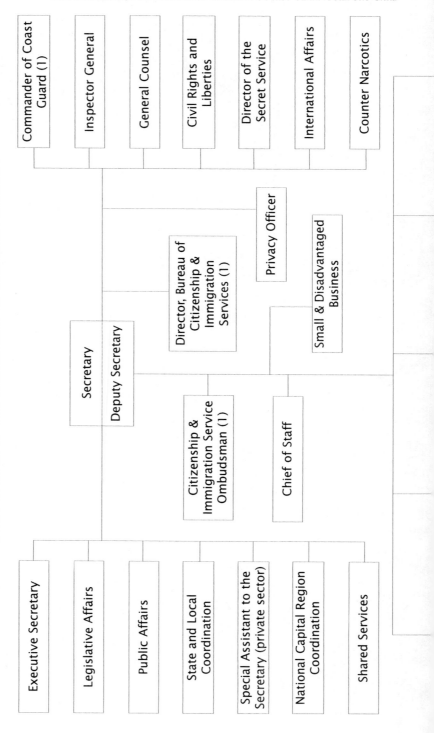

Undersecretary Science and Technology	Undersecretary Management	Undersecretary Information Analysis and Infrastructure Protection	Undersecretary Border and Transportation Security	Undersecretary Emergency Preparedness and Response
♦ Environ. Measures Lab ♦ Nonproliferation & Verification Program ♦ Bio. & Environ. Research Program ♦ Nuclear Assessment Program ♦ Lawrence Livermore National Lab ♦ Bio-Weapons Defense Analysis Center ♦ National Domestic Preparedness Office ♦ Domestic Emergency Support Team ♦ Metro Medical Response Team ♦ National Disaster Medical System ♦ Office of Emergency Preparedness ♦ Strategic National Stockpile ♦ Plum Island Disease Center ♦ NOAA's Integrated Hazard Information	♦ Budget ♦ Appropriations ♦ Expenditure of Funds ♦ Accounting and Finance ♦ Procurement ♦ Human Resources ♦ Information Technology ♦ Facilities ♦ Performance Measurement	Oversight of: ♦ National Infrastructure Protection Center ♦ National Communications System ♦ Critical Infrastructure Assurance Office ♦ National Infrastructure Simulation and Analysis Center ♦ Energy Assurance Office ♦ States Computer Emergency Response Team ♦ Federal Computer Incident Response Center	♦ Office of Domestic Preparedness ♦ Federal Law Enforcement Training Center ♦ US Customs Service ♦ Transportation Security Agency ♦ Immigration and Naturalization Service ♦ Animal and Plant Health Inspection Service ♦ Federal Protective Service	♦ Domestic Emergency Support Team ♦ Strategic National Stockpile ♦ National Disaster Medical Response Team ♦ Nuclear Incident Response Team ♦ Federal Emergency Management Agency

1.

AVIATION SECURITY

E. Marla Felcher

Five weeks after the September 11, 2001, attacks, President Bush signed the Aviation and Transportation Security Act (ATSA), creating the Transportation Security Administration (TSA). Housed within the Department of Transportation, the TSA was responsible for protecting the nation's transportation systems, including aviation, waterways, rails, highways, public transit, and pipelines. Most of the TSA's resources have gone toward securing the aviation system: $4.5 billion of the agency's $4.8 billion budget in fiscal year 2002 was spent on aviation security, as was $6.1 billion of its $7.1 billion budget in fiscal year 2003. The TSA was transferred from the Department of Transportation to the Department of Homeland Security on March 1, 2003. (See Appendix, page 52, for a detailed timeline.)

The nation's aviation system is undoubtedly more secure today than it was on September 11, 2001. During its first year, the TSA made significant progress laying the groundwork for the nation's new security regimen. The agency hired tens of thousands of airport checkpoint screeners, whose job it was to prevent airline passengers from carrying dangerous weapons on board planes. After becoming a DHS agency, the TSA completed background checks on all of those screeners, a measure intended to prevent non-U.S. citizens and people with criminal histories from holding the job.

The TSA also made impressive progress installing equipment in airports to screen passengers' checked luggage. Now, 100 percent of suitcases are screened for explosives, compared to 5 percent prior to the TSA's inception. Significant improvements have been made to the federal air marshal program as well. Previously, the program employed just thirty-three agents; today between four thousand and six thousand undercover agents protect passengers on international and domestic flights. (Their exact number and the flights they are on are both closely guarded secrets.)

Still, much remains to be done. Questions have been raised concerning the adequacy of the checkpoint screeners' training and testing, as well as the TSA's lack of screener performance data. While the agency keeps track of how many dangerous weapons the screeners are intercepting from passengers, it does not have a good handle on how many dangerous weapons screeners are failing to detect. In the past, government studies in which undercover agents attempted to smuggle simulated weapons through security checkpoints found alarmingly high infiltration rates, but a recent General Accounting Office report found that the TSA has done little to measure how effectively screeners detect "threat objects." Undercover tests conducted by people outside the TSA have demonstrated, however, that it is still possible for passengers to carry weapons onto planes.

The TSA has made some, but certainly not enough, progress on its Computer-Assisted Passenger Prescreening System, CAPPS II, a program intended to identify terrorists after they buy an airplane ticket but before they board a plane. After missing multiple deadlines, the TSA estimates CAPPS II will be implemented in the fall of 2005. Another technologically sophisticated program, a Transportation Workers Identification Credential (TWIC), is still in development. TWIC cards will prevent unauthorized people from entering secure areas of airports.

Two important but largely neglected sectors of the aviation industry, air cargo and general aviation (private planes), remain as vulnerable to terrorist attack today as they were on September 11, 2001. Despite repeated warnings from the General Accounting Office, the Department of Transportation inspector general, and members of Congress, the TSA has taken few measures to secure these gaping holes in the aviation security system.

BACKGROUND: BUILDING THE POST–SEPTEMBER 11 AVIATION SECURITY REGIMEN

Congress allocated $2.4 billion for the TSA to get started, and President Bush was quick to appoint John Magaw, a former head of the Secret Service, as the TSA's first leader.[1] The combination of the Aviation and Transportation Security Act's sweeping mandates, Congress's generous budget allocation, and Magaw's law enforcement background sent a strong message that the U.S. government was determined to reform thoroughly and augment aviation security.

Prior to the September 11 terrorist attacks, aviation security was the joint responsibility of the Federal Aviation Administration (FAA) and the airlines. The FAA (a Department of Transportation agency) provided oversight, and the airlines provided and paid for security. There was widespread agreement within the U.S. government that this arrangement had created a system that was not secure. (Poorly trained airport checkpoint screeners, many of whom were not U.S. citizens, were often paid less than workers at airport fast-food restaurants.) There was decidedly less agreement, however, on what it would take to secure the system. The Aviation and Transportation Security Act read like a laundry list of all the security measures Congress and the FAA had contemplated, yet failed to institute, over the past fifteen years.

Transportation Secretary Norman Mineta gave the job of transforming the Aviation and Transportation Security Act's mandates into specific security programs to his deputy, Michael Jackson. Jackson viewed aviation security as a ring of protective layers around an aircraft that would prevent a terrorist attack.[2] Individual security programs would not necessarily keep a terrorist from hijacking or blowing up a plane, but cumulatively the layers would provide adequate protection. Some of the TSA's security programs would keep dangerous *objects* off planes—a new workforce of stringently trained airport checkpoint workers would screen passengers and their carry-on bags, and high-tech explosives detection systems would scan passengers' checked luggage for bombs. Other measures would keep dangerous *people* away from planes—criminal background checks for airport screeners, an airline passenger profiling system capable of flagging terrorists after they bought an airplane ticket but before they boarded a plane, and airport access controls that would keep unauthorized people from entering an airport's secure areas, such as airfields and baggage-handling rooms. The innermost layer of protection, undercover air marshals positioned in first-class seats, would be a last-ditch effort to protect the aircraft's passengers and crew if the outermost layers failed.

The Aviation and Transportation Security Act set forth unambiguous, quantifiable goals for the two layers of the new security regimen Congress deemed most urgent: passenger and luggage screening. Specifically, the TSA was to

- hire, train, and deploy a new federal workforce of airport checkpoint screeners to all of the nation's 429 commercial airports by November 19, 2002, and

- purchase and install explosives-detection systems to scan passengers' checked luggage in all of the nation's 429 commercial airports by December 31, 2002.

Congressional staffers estimated the TSA would need to hire a workforce of twenty-eight thousand airport checkpoint screeners and purchase about one thousand explosives detection systems (costing some $1 million each). The TSA's ability to complete this work within the time frame specified by Congress would become the metric by which its oversight committees, and the American people, would judge its efficacy.

RECOVERING FROM THE SCREENER DEPLOYMENT DEBACLE

TSA chief John Magaw struggled in his new job. When it became clear, very early on, that Congress had grossly underestimated the number of screeners needed to secure airport checkpoints, Magaw appeared before the TSA's House Appropriations Subcommittee on Transportation to ask for more money. Chairman Harold Rogers (R-KY), who had been opposed to federalizing aviation security from the start, set the tone for this and many of the agency's hearings to come. Rogers, along with a number of his Democratic and Republican colleagues in both the House and Senate, chastised Magaw for hiring too many people and running through his budget too quickly.[3] Many feared that the TSA was becoming a bloated government bureaucracy, incapable of meeting its goals.

Six months into his deadline, John Magaw had not deployed federal screeners to a single airport.[4] The TSA chief insisted he would meet his goals, but many in Congress and the White House were pessimistic. At the same time, airline passengers were losing patience with the interim, private workforce screeners who, in their efforts to provide more thorough security, were creating long lines and hour-long waits at airport checkpoints. The airline industry complained that the TSA's first leader was taking the new security drill too far. President Bush did not ignore these concerns; he fired John Magaw in July 2002.[5]

Less than four months later, on November 19, 2002, Secretary Mineta and Admiral James Loy, Magaw's replacement, announced that the TSA had met Congress's deadline and deployed federal screeners to all 429 airports.[6] Forty-four thousand screeners had been hired. It would take another six months for Congress to understand fully the downside of its myopic focus on the TSA's ability to meet hastily formulated benchmarks.

The Aviation and Transportation Security Act required the new federal screeners to undergo background checks to ensure that the TSA employees were not themselves criminals or security threats.[7] Yet, during the first six months of 2003, airline passengers filed more than 6,700 complaints accusing TSA employees of stealing cash, jewelry, and computers.[8] New York City police arrested a number of the TSA screeners for offenses that included possession of drugs and an illegal Mac Ten machine gun. Twelve screeners at the Los Angeles International Airport, who had badges giving them access to secure areas of the airport, were found to have criminal records related to "the unlawful use, sale, distribution or manufacture of an explosive or weapon."[9] By the end of 2003, the TSA had fired more than nineteen hundred airport workers nationwide, at least five hundred of whom had been arrested or convicted of crimes (including rape, manslaughter, and burglary); others had lied on their job applications.[10]

The problem was that criminal background checks were a more complex, time-consuming process than Congress had anticipated. The tens of thousands of applicants who had applied for TSA screener jobs had been given English-language competency, medical, object-recognition, and baggage-lifting tests. Passing these tests initiated the background checks, a process that required the coordination of multiple government agencies, including the FBI, the Immigration and Naturalization Service (INS), the Department of Defense, and the Office of Personnel Management. As of the summer of 2003, the majority of the TSA's checkpoint screeners, thirty thousand employees, had not completed this process.[11] Yet, many had been working in airport jobs for seven months. If the TSA had waited for the background checks to be completed, the agency would have missed Congress's screener deployment deadline.

Background checks were not the only task the TSA officials let fall by the wayside in their rush to deploy tens of thousands of new workers to airports within a year. In September 2003, the General Accounting Office released a report describing the TSA's screener training program as "remedial."[12] A month later, the TSA inspector general reported that most of the questions on the screeners' written test had been rehearsed with the applicants immediately before the exam and that many of the "simplistic" questions were "phrased so as to provide an obvious clue to the correct answer."[13] After reading the exam questions, Senator Charles E. Schumer (D-NY), head of a Democratic Party task force on homeland security, said, "When you read the test, you'd think it was written by [comedian] Jay Leno's scriptwriters rather than by a testing agency."[14]

Despite the deficiencies in the screeners' training and testing, it is nonetheless possible that the new TSA employees would have been capable of performing the job they had been hired to do: keeping passengers from carrying dangerous objects onto planes. Ultimately, this is the only performance measure that matters. Press releases issued by the TSA suggest that the screeners are in fact passing this on-the-job test with flying colors. During its first year in business, the TSA reported, checkpoint screeners intercepted more than 4.8 million prohibited items, including 1,101 firearms, nearly 1.4 million knives, 2.4 million sharp objects, 40,000 box cutters, 125,000 flammable objects, and 15,700 clubs.[15] In August 2003, TSA lauded its screeners for confiscating "artfully concealed items," including a handgun stuffed inside a plush teddy bear, a child's car seat that was used to conceal a knife, and a "statue artifact" concealing a sword.[16]

There is no doubt that air travel is safer when vigilant screeners prevent passengers from boarding planes with handguns, knives, and

swords. But the measure offered by the TSA—the number of prohibited items detected—tells just part of the story. Assessing the extent to
which screeners have improved aviation security requires the agency
to answer one more question: *How many dangerous objects are
screeners failing to detect and intercept?* According to the September
2003 General Accounting Office report, no one knows.[17] "TSA currently collects little information," the GAO said, "to measure screener
performance in detecting threat objects."[18]

While there may be a dearth of screener performance data
from the TSA itself, several news organizations and at least one
private citizen have conducted their own screener tests. The results
are not encouraging. On Labor Day weekend 2002, a team of
New York *Daily News* reporters got carry-on bags packed with
pepper spray, rubber-handled razor knives, box cutters, and razor
blades onto planes in eleven airports.[19] In July 2003, WBNS News
in Ohio hired former FAA undercover agent Steve Elson to see if
he could get lead-lined film bags through airport security.[20] The
lead lining, intended to protect film from being damaged by X-ray
machines, also shields the bags' contents from screeners. Because
a weapon concealed in such a bag would appear as a big black
blob, screeners are instructed to search these carry-on bags by
hand. The first time Elson passed through security, the TSA
screener correctly followed protocol: he opened the bag, hand-
searched its contents, and sent it through the X-ray machine twice.
Yet, subsequent tests were disappointing; at three different checkpoints, screeners failed to inspect the lead-lined bags by hand.
Then, in October 2003, a college student stashed box cutters and
other dangerous items on four Southwest Airlines planes, where
they sat for weeks before they were discovered. The student claimed
his goal was to bring public attention to what he perceived to be
ongoing lapses in security.[21]

The TSA officials described the media tests as "unrealistic" and
"alarmist" and denied that they are an accurate measure of screener
performance. In response to the college student's actions, the TSA
deputy administrator Steven McHale said, "Amateur testing like this
does not in any way assist us or show us where we have flaws in our
system."[22] The agency announced, however, that it had recently completed a "screener performance improvement study" and is "taking
steps to address [performance measurement] deficiencies identified"
by the General Accounting Office.[23]

CONTRACTOR OVERSIGHT AND COST CONTROLS:
CLAIMS OF IMPROVEMENT AFTER A BAD START

As a brand-new agency, the TSA did not have an adequate workforce in place to build an organization and implement a host of new aviation security programs simultaneously. Some employees had been transferred to the TSA from the FAA, but there were still hundreds of staff jobs to be filled and tens of thousands of airport workers to hire. The only chance the new agency had of meeting Congress's deadlines was to rely heavily on private sector contractors to do the bulk of its early work. The Department of Transportation awarded $8.5 billion to contractors in 2002, among them, Lockheed Martin ($370 million for checkpoint "lane reconfiguration"), VF Solutions ($17 million for TSA screener uniforms), Boeing ($508 million for explosives detection machines), Accenture ($215 million for ongoing human resources support), and NCS Pearson ($103 million to recruit the screeners).[24] The combination of the TSA's tight deadlines, Congress's initially generous budget allocation, and lax contractor oversight became a recipe for wasteful spending and contractor billing abuses.

During the first few months, when the TSA was getting organized, the FAA legal and purchasing staff helped the TSA award contracts to the interim screening companies that would operate between November 2001, when the Aviation and Transportation Security Act became law, and November 2002, when the TSA had hired its own screener workforce. During this time, the FAA entered into agreements with seventy-four companies, obligating the TSA to spend $1 billion.[25] Rushing to get the job done, the FAA staff did not have time to negotiate the contracts. Instead, they issued "letter contracts" stipulating that the contractors would bill the TSA about what they had charged the airlines for screeners in 2000. Yet, half of the contractors reneged on this promise and ultimately charged the TSA between 50 and 100 percent more than the amount they had charged the airlines a year earlier, accounting for at least $300 million in overcharges.[26]

The TSA also was overcharged by the contractor responsible for hiring the screener workforce, NCS Pearson. One reason for the delay in screener background checks was NCS Pearson's sudden departure after the company's initial $103.4 million contract had ballooned inexplicably to $700 million.[27] Government auditors eventually learned that Pearson had billed the TSA more than $5 million for New York–area screeners to live for up to six months in hotels and for recruiters to stay for stretches of weeks at a time at luxury resort hotels in Florida, the Virgin Islands, Colorado, and Hawaii.[28]

In the summer of 2003, Loy reported that the TSA had made considerable progress creating the systems it needed to monitor the costs and performance of its contractors and that the situation would continue to improve.[29]

PROGRESS ON INSPECTING CHECKED LUGGAGE

Congress mandated the TSA to install explosives detection systems in every U.S. airport to screen each piece of checked baggage by December 2002. The agency made an impressive effort to meet this deadline but was ultimately unable to do so. The major hurdles were funding and space; Congress did not allocate enough money for airports to integrate the explosives detection systems into their baggage-handling systems, and many airports did not have anywhere to put the minivan-sized machines. The Homeland Security Act extended the TSA's baggage-screening deadline and gave the agency the authority to implement "alternate screening methods" for up to another year. Among the methods that the TSA approved to replace the explosives detection systems temporarily were trace detection machines (a cotton swab is run across the outside of luggage and tested for traces of explosive chemicals), bomb-sniffing dogs, and physical searches.[30] Although the TSA came close to making the extended December 2003 deadline, it did not make that one either; explosives detection systems are still not installed in five airports.[31]

Airport operators continue to complain that their efforts to integrate explosives detection systems equipment into baggage-handling systems are being thwarted by Congress's reluctance to allocate enough money for them to get the job done. Many of the machines remain in airport lobbies, requiring screeners to take the checked luggage from passengers, run the suitcases through the explosives detection machines, and then transport them to baggage-handling rooms. What prevents this labor-intensive process from being mechanized is money; it will cost airports between $1 million and $3 million to integrate each explosives detection machine into their baggage-handling systems. So far, the TSA has promised seven airports a total of $700 million to get the job done and has identified another twenty-five to thirty-five airports as candidates for integration. But until Congress authorizes the funding, the work cannot begin, and the machines will remain in airport lobbies.

Despite these infrastructure problems, there is good news: according to a recent Department of Transportation inspector general investigation, all checked bags are now being screened for explosives in some way.[32] This is an impressive accomplishment for the TSA, given that before the agency existed, only 5 percent of checked luggage was inspected.

IMPROVEMENTS IN THE OUTER- AND INNERMOST LAYERS OF SECURITY

The TSA deserves additional credit for making some progress in several other realms, including passenger profiling, air marshals, and airport perimeter and access controls:

COMPUTER-ASSISTED PASSENGER PRESCREENING SYSTEM: CAPPS II

The TSA's passenger profiling via the Computer-Assisted Passenger Prescreening System (CAPPS II) is considered by many security experts to be the most important layer of its "system of systems." CAPPS II will integrate vast amounts of information on every airline passenger, including demographic data (name, date of birth, address) and information held by other government agencies such as the INS and the FBI, to compute a passenger "risk score." Airport screeners will use the score to determine the level of scrutiny to which each passenger will be subjected before being allowed to board a plane.

The CAPPS II deadline, originally set for June 2004, has been moved to the fall of 2005, owing in large part to the unexpected level of public criticism over the TSA's ambitious data collection efforts and their privacy implications. An early prototype of the CAPPS II program gave the TSA access to what was considered by some to be too much personal information, including where passengers had lived in the past, who their neighbors had been, the charities to which they had donated money, to whom they had been married and for how long, and details of their health and financial histories. The American Civil Liberties Union and the National Association for the Advancement of Colored People were among the many organizations objecting to the scope of the information to be collected by the TSA, how long it would be stored in government computers, and who would get to see it.[33]

In response, the TSA scaled back its data collection plans. In September 2003, the agency announced that financial and health information would not be part of the profiling database, as was the TSA's original plan. The agency also promised that passenger data would be purged within a few days of the flight being finished and that private companies involved in the data collection process would be prohibited from retaining the output in a "commercially usable form."[34] The original CAPPS II plan would have allowed the TSA to keep some information for up to fifty years.

Privacy advocates were cautiously optimistic after the TSA announced these safeguards. But in September 2003, a blunder by three-year-old discount airline, JetBlueAirways, demonstrated that airline passengers had a right to be concerned about losing control of their personal data. The airline acknowledged that it had given the Pentagon information on 5 million of its passengers without their consent, including their names, addresses, and phone numbers.[35] The Pentagon, in turn, passed the information to a private sector contractor who had used it to identify passengers' Social Security numbers, occupation, income, home- and car-ownership history, as well as the number of adults and children living in the passenger's household. The Pentagon intended to use the data for research on its own "airline passenger risk assessment" system.[36] The airline's indiscretion rekindled an intense level of public outrage, including various class-action lawsuits filed against JetBlue on behalf of its passengers.

JetBlue had shared its data with the Pentagon, not with the TSA. But which federal agency was responsible was of little concern to those who felt their privacy had been invaded. This point did not go unnoticed by the airlines, whose participation the TSA very much needs to continue testing CAPPS II. As of the end of 2003, the agency had not been able to convince a single airline to hand over its passenger data for a CAPPS II pilot program.[37] The debate over passenger privacy was ratcheted up another notch in January 2004, when Northwest Airlines acknowledged that it had provided the National Aeronautics and Space Administration three months of its passengers' reservation information shortly after the September 11 attacks, despite the airline's previous claims that it had never given such information to anyone.[38]

Acting TSA administrator David M. Stone has the authority to force the airlines give him their data by issuing a security directive, similar to orders the agency issues to airports and airlines when security is heightened. Stone says this is exactly what he intends to do if the airlines do not agree to participate voluntarily.[39]

In November 2003, the General Accounting Office's director of homeland security and justice, Cathleen A. Berrick, testified before the House Committee on Government Reform on the state of the CAPPS II system. Berrick[40] reported that the many challenges the TSA is currently facing with CAPPS II—how to ensure the accuracy of CAPPS II data, how to redress erroneous information, and how to prevent a "high-risk" person from stealing someone else's identity and subsequently boarding a plane—in fact may impede significantly the agency's ability to implement the system. The GAO is in the midst of an extensive CAPPS II investigation and expects to release its findings in 2004.

FEDERAL AIR MARSHALS

On September 11, 2001, the U.S. federal air marshal program employed just thirty-three undercover agents, whose job it was to prevent hijackings on U.S. commercial aircraft. The program's budget, about $4 million a year, covered only a handful of international flights; the twenty thousand domestic flights that took off from domestic airports each day were unprotected by the highly trained agents.[41]

By the summer of 2002, the TSA had hired between four and six thousand new undercover air marshals (the exact number is classified information), who were to guard the cockpits of both international and domestic flights, typically from first-class seats.[42] Congress had given the TSA $1 billion to resuscitate the program. Although the program had been well funded, there were still problems. Lured from jobs with police departments, U.S. Customs, and the Border Patrol, the new agents found that the reality of their workday fell short of what the TSA recruiters had promised. The program was disorganized, many marshals complained, the training was inadequate, and twelve- and sixteen-hour workdays sitting on planes were simultaneously monotonous and exhausting. During one eighteen-day period in the summer of 2002, 1,250 unhappy marshals called in sick. By the end of the month, at least 250 had quit.[43]

TSA chief Loy worked with Department of Homeland Security officials to find a solution. By September 2003, they had settled on a plan: air marshals were to be transferred out of the TSA and into the Bureau of Immigration and Customs Enforcement, a new Department of Homeland Security agency.[44] Immigration agents, customs officers, and air marshals would be cross-trained to perform all three jobs. The move would more than double the number of air marshals to eleven thousand by creating a system of "reserve" agents who would be placed on planes only when the Department of Homeland Security perceived an increased threat to aviation security. The new plan was a step toward improving air marshal morale. But the move had broader long-term implications: transferring the air marshal program out of the TSA demonstrated the Department of Homeland Security's ability to respond to a difficult problem quickly and to implement a solution that resulted in a more efficient use of agency resources.

AIRPORT PERIMETERS AND ACCESS CONTROLS

The Aviation and Transportation Security Act required airports to strengthen the security of their perimeters, airfields, jetways, and baggage-handling rooms. The TSA has made some progress in this area; airports have decreased the number of perimeter access points; individuals and vehicles are randomly stopped and searched at entry points; and criminal history checks have been completed for most airport workers. In October 2003, the agency awarded a contract to Unisys to test and evaluate technologies the TSA is considering for a TWIC. The card will use biometric technologies, possibly fingerprints and retinal scans, to identify airport employees and keep unauthorized people out of airports' secure areas. The card will serve as a common credential for the 12 million workers in the nation's transportation systems.

Yet, as airports continue to improve the security of their "sterile" areas, new security vulnerabilities continue to surface. In November 2002, terrorists believed to be associated with al Qaeda shot two SA-7 shoulder-fired missiles at an Israeli passenger jet shortly after it took off from Mombasa, Kenya. The missiles narrowly missed hitting the plane, raising concerns within the United States that the weapons would someday be used against an American target. Airport officials have become increasingly worried about the highly portable missiles being launched from locations near or in airports. Airport directors report that they have increased their surveillance of perimeters but continue to voice concerns to the TSA about their inability to guard completely against this threat. Motion detectors, closed-circuit televisions, and barriers are among the measures that are available but have not yet been used to secure and monitor airport perimeters. The problem is money: Congress has failed to fund adequately programs that would improve airport perimeter security. While the TSA continues to study alternative solutions, the question, "Who will pay?" remains unanswered.

GAPING HOLES THAT REMAIN IN THE NATION'S AVIATION SECURITY NET: GENERAL AVIATION AND AIR CARGO

GENERAL AVIATION: PRIVATE PLANES

There are about 219,000 privately owned planes in the U.S. general aviation fleet, ranging from two-seaters to 737 jets.[45] Recreational flyers, sports teams, cropdusters, banner advertisers, aerial sightseeing companies, and corporate executives are among the diverse users of general aviation planes. Single-engine propeller planes account for about 70 percent of the fleet. These small planes can take off and land anywhere, including the nation's commercial airports and an additional 2,500 public-use airports designated specifically for general aviation. Pilots also can fly from their own private airstrips, built on farms and even in backyards. On any given day in the United States, there are about 132,000 general aviation flights in the sky.

Private pilot and security consultant Joseph A. Kinney wrote in a *Washington Post* editorial[46] shortly after the September 11 attacks that anyone who has visited a general aviation facility knows that security ranges between poor and nonexistent. It took a suicidal teenager, fourteen-year-old Charles J. Bishop, to point up just how easy it is, even in today's America, to steal a small plane. On January 5, 2002, Bishop flew a four-seat Cessna into the twenty-eighth floor of the forty-two-story Bank of America building in Tampa, killing himself but injuring no one else.[47]

Two years after Bishop's crash, the TSA has taken little action to improve general aviation security. General aviation pilots are still not required to pass through airport security screening, nor are their passengers, suitcases, or cargo. That is why the General Accounting Office concluded in April 2003, and again the following November, that general aviation is far more vulnerable than commercial aviation to terrorist attack.[48] Yet, neither Congress nor the TSA has imposed any regulations on private planes that would prevent a terrorist from replicating Bishop's flight, this time with a plane loaded with explosives. The TSA officials, who have referred to the general aviation industry as "unregulated," report that the agency does not plan to impose any rules on private planes in the foreseeable future.[49]

The Aircraft Operators and Pilots Association, a lobbying group representing about 398,000 private plane owners and pilots, applauds Congress's and the TSA's hands-off stance.[50] The organization has many congressional allies and benefactors, chief among them Representative James L. Oberstar (D-MN), who counts the lobbying group among his top campaign contributors.[51] In March 2003, Oberstar introduced a House proposal to commend the organization on its "proactive commitment to the security of general aviation."[52] In fact, the association has battled regulators on most general aviation security measures considered after September 11, including airspace restrictions over major cities during heightened terrorist alerts, the ban of small planes at Washington's Reagan National Airport, restrictions on banner-towing advertising over stadiums, a bill requiring general aviation pilots to pass criminal background checks, and another measure requiring FBI checks for flight school operators.[53]

General aviation industry officials maintain that there has never been a terrorist attack involving a private plane, therefore it is unnecessary for the government to impose new security regulations. For now, Congress and the TSA agree.

AIR CARGO

Last year, more than 12 million tons of cargo and mail were transported by air in the United States. About 75 percent of air cargo is shipped on cargo-only planes. The rest, about 3 million tons annually, flies on commercial flights, in the holds of planes along with passengers' suitcases.[54] The TSA estimates there is a 35 to 65 percent chance that terrorists are planning to place a bomb in the cargo of a U.S. passenger plane. Yet, only about 5 percent of air cargo is screened, even if it is transported on passenger planes.[55] Congress did not legislate new security initiatives for the air cargo industry in the Aviation and Transportation Security Act. Instead, the TSA was given a mandate only to "ensure the adequacy of security measures for the transportation of cargo," stopping short of specifying how cargo should be inspected and holding the TSA to no firm deadline. The result: cargo, whether carried aboard cargo-only or commercial passenger flights, continues to be highly vulnerable to terrorists' bombs, the General Accounting Office reported in November 2003.[56]

Industry executives are pessimistic about the government's ability to come up with an effective air cargo security plan, largely because of the degree to which their business relies on speed. The success of air cargo companies is closely tied to their ability to move highly perishable and valuable goods across the world at a moment's notice. Enhanced security can only slow down companies' tightly scheduled operations.

Some members of Congress have attempted to fill in the air cargo security gap, while others are intent on making sure the industry is not saddled with any new regulations. Senators Kay Bailey Hutchison (R-TX) and Dianne Feinstein (D-CA) introduced an air cargo security bill in January 2003, which was passed by the Senate in May 2003.[57] The bill calls for the TSA to create a system for the regular inspection of air cargo facilities and for every cargo shipper to develop a security plan, subject to the TSA's approval. The Hutchison-Feinstein bill has moved to the House, but Representative Don Young (R-AK), chairman of the Transportation and Infrastructure Committee, has refused to mark it up. Young has come up with a competing bill that calls only for the TSA to create a cargo-screening pilot program that assesses "the capabilities of the private sector."[58]

In September 2003, House and Senate negotiators rejected a spending bill provision that would have required the TSA to develop a plan for screening air cargo carried aboard passenger planes. The reason, said a House Appropriations Committee spokesperson, was that screening technology does not yet exist. Representative Edward J. Markey (D-MA) disagreed and blamed congressional Republicans for eliminating the provision because the air cargo industry opposed it.[59]

James Loy had the authority to force airlines and air cargo companies to institute specific security measures, just as he had the authority to force the airlines to hand over their passengers' personal data for CAPPS II. But he refused to do so. Instead, Loy passed the issue to the Aviation Security Advisory Committee, a group of government and industry representatives pulled together by the FAA in 1989 (in the wake of the Pan Am Flight 103 bombing) to counsel regulators. While under the jurisdiction of the FAA, the advisory committee, dominated by the aviation industry, had a thirteen-year history of stalling or thwarting every security-related regulation the airlines opposed.[60]

The Aviation Security Advisory Committee met in October 2003 to make its cargo security recommendations.[61] The next step is for the TSA to turn these suggestions into a proposed regulation. Industry then will have an opportunity to comment on the TSA's proposal, a process that can take months. It will be up to the TSA staff to decide how to integrate industry's ideas and concerns into the final cargo security regulation—a process that often took years at the FAA. The TSA has set no firm deadline for when a new regulation is likely to go into effect. This is the same course followed by most security regulations the FAA considered prior to 2001, a script that ultimately resulted in the promulgation of few security regulations and an aviation system highly vulnerable to terrorist attack.

THE FUTURE OF U.S. DOMESTIC AVIATION SECURITY

On September 11, 1989, security expert Robert Kupperman of the Center for Strategic and International Studies addressed the Senate Governmental Affairs Committee. "The problem with terrorism is its episodic nature," he said. "During the periods of relative calm, terrorism is viewed by large governments, including our own, as a minor annoyance . . . and it is difficult to get the policy levels of government focused on the problem at all. But when an incident occurs, particularly one dominated by media coverage, terrorism takes on a virtual strategic significance. When terrorists strike, governments go on hold, paralyzed by an unfolding human drama, which is televised for all to see."[62] After an attack, Kupperman told the group of senators, there is a groundswell of support for measures that would prevent it from occurring again, but ultimately this enthusiasm dissipates and little changes.

Kupperman's observations were an apt description of the "aviation disaster script" that played out in the following years, specifically, the 1988 bombing of a Pan Am 747 over Lockerbie, Scotland, and the 1996 explosion of a TWA 747 off the coast of New York.[63] The FAA staff and officials, the Department of Transportation inspector general, government task forces, congressional oversight committees, White House commissions, and the General Accounting Office identified, investigated, documented, and offered solutions intended to prevent disaster from occurring again. Between 1988 and 2001, the GAO issued more than forty reports warning that lax security in the nation's airports left our airports and planes highly vulnerable to terrorist attack. The Department of Transportation inspector general's office issued dozens more reports, all saying essentially the same thing. Two presidents, George H. W. Bush and Bill Clinton, convened blue-ribbon commissions to study the problem. Both groups seconded the opinions of the General Accounting Office and Department of Transportation inspector general that security was abysmal. These investigations and reports culminated with interminable congressional hearings, much passing of the buck, and few security enhancements.

That Congress refused to take any action to improve aviation security in light of indisputable evidence that U.S. aircraft were an easy target for terrorists, was attributable primarily to the airlines' tenacious efforts to delay, dilute, or defeat every measure that threatened their short-term pecuniary interests. Security was viewed as an expense, not a revenue-generating line item, and they did not want to spend the money. Therefore, each time Congress even considered security-related legislation, the aviation industry would respond by dispatching its representatives to Capitol Hill. Reinforcing the lobbyists' efforts were the airlines' open checkbooks: between 1990 and

2000 the air transport industry donated more than $67 million to politicians' campaigns.[64]

WHY SECURITY IS BETTER TODAY THAN IT WAS ON SEPTEMBER 11, 2001

The September 11 terrorists finally motivated Congress to enact legislation that improved the nation's aviation security. That the government would be picking up the tab for aviation security quelled the airlines' objections, at least temporarily. The result: aviation security is stronger now than it has ever been in the nation's history. There are more screeners stationed at airport checkpoints than ever before, and they are better paid and more experienced than their private sector predecessors; screeners' annual attrition rate has dropped to about 14 percent, from between 100 and 400 percent when they were considered by the airlines to be little more than a line-item expense. While the adequacy of the screeners' training and testing has been rightly questioned, the overall caliber of the workforce certainly has been raised. All of the screener background checks pending as of the summer of 2003 have been completed, and screeners with questionable backgrounds have been fired.[65] Backing up the screeners' efforts are the 1,060 explosives detection systems and 5,300 electronic trace detectors that scan 100 percent of passengers' luggage for explosives.

Two innermost layers of the "system of systems" now decrease the probability of a terrorist gaining control of a plane in midair: airport cockpit doors have been reinforced to prevent intruders from gaining access to the flight deck, and thousands of undercover air marshals fly on tens of thousands of domestic and international flights each month to protect the planes' passengers and crew.

Although a final version of CAPPS II has not been implemented, the TSA has joined efforts with U.S. and international intelligence agencies to do a better job of flagging suspected terrorists at airports. In August 2003, airline ticket agents at the Seattle-Tacoma International Airport alerted police after the names of two passengers appeared on a "no-fly" list the TSA had circulated to the airlines. This would not have occurred before the TSA. In fact, on September 11, 2001, the

FAA's "no-fly" list was three hundred names long and contained the names of two of the hijackers. But the FAA had not circulated the list to the airlines because, according to one FAA official, "We just never got around to setting up a protocol for who would control the list and how we would get the airlines to implement it."[66]

In fiscal year 2001, the FAA spent $160.4 million on aviation security; the TSA spent $4.5 billion on aviation security in FY 2002 and will spend at least $6.1 billion more in FY 2003. While Congress and the TSA have allowed two enormous security gaps to remain, air cargo and general aviation, most of the holes that existed in the system two years ago have been made significantly smaller.

THE TRADE-OFFS CONNECTED TO SECURITY

Despite these improvements, there is a limit to how far the TSA can be expected to raise the bar, given that the Aviation and Transportation Security Act did not get at the root of the aviation security problem—our government's reluctance to view security along a continuum rather than as an absolute. Each point along the continuum represents a series of trade-offs affected by the level of security our leaders choose for the country, including aviation industry profitability, costs to the government, passenger convenience, and privacy. Before the TSA came into being, the aviation system operated far to one side of this continuum, "low security," as Congress hesitated to mandate any security enhancement that would saddle either the U.S. government or the airlines with millions of dollars of new expenses. Refusing to act, Congress tried to wish away the risk of a terrorist attack on America's aviation system.

This trade-off had advantages for passengers as well as the government and the airlines. Travelers moved freely throughout airports, checkpoint lines remained short, invasive searches of our bodies and luggage were rare, airline tickets remained free of security taxes, and, in the absence of a profiling system like CAPPS II, privacy remained intact. For many years, the interests of passengers, Congress, and the airline industry appeared to be aligned under this "low-security" policy.

Then, in a flash, the 2001 attacks jolted us to the opposite end of the security continuum. Suddenly, we were demanding high levels of security. In response, Congress enacted sweeping legislation in record time, allocating an unprecedented amount of money for the TSA to fix what was now an obviously broken system. In an abrupt about-face, our leaders adopted a "zero-risk" mentality, promising to spare no expense to do all that was necessary to secure our planes. No public official would have dared to explain that, while the nation's new security regimen was capable of decreasing the probability of another attack, it would certainly not lower the risk to zero. The public needed to be assured that it was safe to fly, and the notion of "zero risk" was what they needed to get back in the air. "Public support is much greater, no matter how unrealistic, when there are promises that the risk will be completely eliminated," wrote Harvard University economists Kip Viscusi and Richard Zeckhauser.[67] Cadres of professionally uniformed TSA screeners who combed through our carry-on bags with a level of vigor we had never before witnessed went far to reinforce the proposition that it was once again safe to fly.

This zero-risk mentality is as unsustainable as our pre–September 11 low-security policy. Eventually, Congress and the American public will be forced to confront the fact that there simply is not enough money to fund every security program, nor is it possible to eliminate the risk of another terrorist attack completely. This is the point at which TSA finds itself today. Until now, the agency has directed most of its energy toward organizational and tactical issues. The first year was devoted to hiring, training, and deploying tens of thousands of new employees to airports and to purchasing and installing explosives detection systems. The second year was spent largely on refining what was already in motion (for example, the air marshal program), cleaning up what had gone wrong (airport screener background checks and contractor oversight), and making headway on programs not subject to deadlines (CAPPS II and airport perimeter controls). Now that the TSA is in its third year, the agency, Congress, and the American people must wrestle with a question of longer-term, strategic importance, namely, *how much security do we need, and what are we willing to give up to have it?*

Before our abrupt quest for tight security, many Americans were not even aware of what they were "getting" in return for lax security. It was not until airport checkpoint lines curled around corners and extended out airport doors, guards with machine guns patrolled airport lounges, a security tax appeared on airline tickets, and our privacy was threatened that we even considered the costs associated with heightened security. Legislators' enthusiasm for aviation security had always fizzled long before such changes occurred. The Aviation and Transportation Security Act ensured that these changes would occur. Now, for the first time in history, Americans are aware of what we must give up to have an aviation system terrorists cannot easily penetrate.

In May 2003, Department of Transportation inspector general Kenneth Mead testified before the National Commission on Terrorist Attacks Upon the United States. "The new security model is much more likely to ensure strong aviation security than its predecessor," he concluded after detailing the progress the TSA had made over the previous eighteen months. "However, a cautionary note is in order. The sense of vigilance for a priority attached to tight security can dissipate with the passage of time," the inspector general warned, just as Kupperman had done in 1989, "which in turn may lead to a sense of complacency as well as pressures to relax security."[68] The Aviation and Transportation Security Act brought improvement to security in the United States, but, as Mead pointed out, it did not guarantee that the momentum will continue in the absence of another terrorist attack. And it certainly did not eliminate the source of the most intense "pressures to relax security"—the airline industry. Aviation security is still very much a work in progress. The TSA's to-do list represents an open invitation for the agency's most powerful stakeholder, the airlines, to water down the agency's policies.

When President Eisenhower signed the Federal Aviation Act in 1958, creating the FAA, the agency's dual mission was explicit: ensure aviation safety and promote the aviation industry. At the time, few questions were asked about the ability of a single agency to carry out two missions that could easily collide. Over the next four decades plenty of questions were asked, particularly in the wake of high-profile plane crashes that killed many people. The FAA was stripped of its explicit mandate to promote the aviation industry in 1996, under the Clinton administration. But as long as commercial aviation occupies a central role in the U.S. economy, generating hundreds of billions of dollars annually and accounting for hundreds of thousands of jobs, the issue will not disappear.

Congress's obstinate ambivalence on the security/commerce dichotomy is apparent in the TSA's mission statement today:

The Transportation Security Administration protects the Nation's transportation systems to ensure freedom of movement for people and commerce.[69]

Going forward, it will be up to the TSA's leaders, Congress, and the American people to calibrate just how freely people and commerce should move and the costs and risks they are willing to incur for this freedom.

APPENDIX

TIMELINE OF SIGNIFICANT EVENTS IN THE TSA'S HISTORY

November 19, 2001	President Bush signs Aviation and Transportation Security Act into law
December 10, 2001	President Bush nominates John M. Magaw as undersecretary of transportation security
April 30, 2002	Transportation Security Administration deploys first two hundred checkpoint screeners to Baltimore-Washington International Airport
July 1, 2002	TSA deploys thousands of new federal air marshals to fly on U.S. planes
July 18, 2002	John M. Magaw resigns, replaced by James M. Loy
August 7, 2002	DOT inspector general testifies to House that TSA is having difficulty hiring enough checkpoint screeners
November 18, 2002	TSA meets Congress's screener deployment deadline
December 20, 2002	GAO issues report describing air cargo as vulnerable to terrorist attack

December 31, 2002	TSA meets deadline to screen all checked luggage for explosives[*]
February 28, 2003	DOT inspector general audit finds that TSA contractors overcharged the agency by millions of dollars
March 1, 2003	TSA moved to Department of Homeland Security
April 9, 2003	Airlines complete reinforcement of all aircraft cockpit doors
May 22, 2003	DOT inspector general urges TSA to improve air cargo security and to measure screener performance
July 7, 2003	DHS allocates total of $350 million to three airports for integration of explosive detection systems into baggage-handling systems
September 2, 2003	Federal air marshal program moved to Bureau of Immigration and Customs Enforcement
September 2, 2003	DHS allocates total of $425 million to three more airports for integration of explosives detection machines into baggage-handling systems

[*]While Admiral James Loy announced that the TSA had met its congressional deadline to screen all checked baggage for explosives, this was technically not true. The Aviation and Transportation Security Act mandated the TSA to screen suitcases with electronic explosives detection systems, yet the TSA was not able to buy and install all of the equipment by December 31, 2002. A few months earlier, when it had become clear that the TSA would not be able to meet this deadline, Congress had extended it and approved other screening technologies to be used in the interim, including trace detection machines and bomb-sniffing dogs.

September 24, 2003	TSA approves total of $100 million to reimburse fifty-eight carriers for reinforcing cockpit doors
October 1, 2003	TSA completes all outstanding background checks on airport checkpoint screeners
October 1, 2003	TSA's Aviation Security Advisory Committee offers forty recommendations on how to improve air cargo security
October 16, 2003	TSA awards contract for pilot project to strengthen secure-area access controls at twenty airports
October 23, 2003	TSA administrator James Loy nominated as deputy secretary at Department of Homeland Security
November 17, 2003	TSA releases Air Cargo Strategic Plan
December 4, 2003	Rear Admiral David M. Stone appointed acting administrator of TSA

2.

INTELLIGENCE GATHERING, ANALYSIS, AND SHARING

Gregory F. Treverton

An irony lies at the core of the work on intelligence at the Department of Homeland Security (DHS): when Congress brought together twenty-two different agencies involved in homeland security, it left out the federal government's intelligence operations. The strongest argument for creating the department was to improve the government's ability to coordinate and integrate information available to different agencies to prevent terrorism, yet this proved to be the one big issue that restructuring did not attempt to solve. The Central Intelligence Agency (CIA), the Federal Bureau of Investigation (FBI), and the National Security Agency, as well as the intelligence operations of the departments of Defense and State, all retained their independence. The scramble to respond to the attacks of September 11, 2001, has been something of a free-for-all, and the overlaps in intelligence roles between the Department of Homeland Security and other agencies remain to be sorted out.

Instead of giving the DHS the responsibility for "connecting the dots" of possible threats to the homeland, the administration created a Terrorist Threat Integration Center (TTIC, pronounced "T-Tick"), which reports to the head of the CIA. The DHS and the FBI share the task of reaching out to state and local officials to collect and share information (see Table 2.1, page 56).

TABLE 2.1
DHS AND OTHER AGENCIES INVOLVED IN HOMELAND SECURITY INTELLIGENCE

Office of Information Analysis	Information Analysis and Infrastructure Protection Directorate, DHS	Evolving, but primarily tactical and operational, connected to protecting critical national infra-structures, such as transport, communica-tions, and air traffic
Terrorist Threat Information Center (TTIC)	Reports to the Director of Central Intelligence	"Connecting the dots" of information from all sources to assess the terorist threat, especially to the homeland
Counterterrorism Center (CTC)	CIA, a portion now colocated with TTIC	Primarily operational, providing intelligence in support of counter-terrorism operations abroad
Counterterrorism Division (CTD)	FBI, a portion now colocated with TTIC	Primarily operational, generating domestic intelligence both to prevent terrorist acts and prosecute terrorists
Office of Intelligence	FBI	Evolving, but both pro-viding guidance to operating divisions and field offices in collecting information and analyzing information from those sources

Overall, although a lot has been done, there is much more to do. Assembling the DHS from its inherited pieces has been an enormous task, and neither the department as a whole nor its intelligence function—where given the continued independence of the older intelligence agencies there was very little to inherit—is yet up to speed. The intelligence challenges are hard, especially given the legacy of cold war institutions and processes. The technology issues are perplexing, and the policy ones even more so. More generally, the nation has only begun to figure out what domestic intelligence it wants to gather, and how to do so without infringing on the privacy, or the rights, of its citizens. So far, the Terrorist Threat Integration Center is off to a decent start, the FBI has embarked on a momentous change in mission—from law enforcement to terrorism prevention and intelligence—while remaining hampered by outmoded technology, and the DHS is struggling to get into the game.

SIGNS OF GENUINE PROGRESS

Established early in 2003, the DHS's Information Analysis and Infrastructure Protection Directorate has attracted committed people from around the government and outside it. It publishes warnings affecting various types of infrastructure (information, air transport, finance), based on its inheritance of the National Infrastructure Protection Center, formerly part of the FBI. A handful of its analysts work at the TTIC, alongside those from other intelligence agencies. The TTIC prepares the Presidential Terrorism Threat Report, a highly classified assessment of the latest developments that is sent to the president six times a week.

AREAS OF MINOR TO MODEST PROGRESS

Apart from the infrastructure warnings, the information analysis arm of the DHS's Information Analysis and Infrastructure Protection Directorate has yet to carve out a clear mission and base of "customers," in part because it has not had clear or consistent leadership.

Its first assistant secretary, the famed CIA spy-catcher Paul Redmond, served for only a few months. He was replaced in November 2003 by another intelligence veteran, former Defense Intelligence Agency director General Patrick Hughes. The DHS's broader threat assessment mandate has effectively been ceded to TTIC, and it remains uncertain how tightly the DHS's intelligence will be coupled to its infrastructure-protection mission. The DHS has no authority to collect information, though it has the opportunity to assign other agencies to do that; its own assessments are dependent on information and analysis produced by others. As a result, the thrust of its reports is very operational in nature, focused on the law enforcement and "first responders" (police officers, firefighters, paramedics) who would be first on the scene to help deal with any terrorist act. It does not ask questions like "whither al Qaeda?" but instead concentrates on understanding specific threats to networks or centers of commerce, transportation, or governance and how they might be reduced.

WHERE LITTLE PROGRESS HAS BEEN MADE

Good intentions notwithstanding, sharing information in any consistent way, especially with state and local officials, is still far from reality. As a Markle Foundation task force put it: "DHS has yet to articulate a vision of how it will link federal, state, and local agencies in a communications and sharing network, or what its role will be with respect to the TTIC and other federal agencies."[1] There is no gainsaying the difficulty of the task. Not only is infrastructure for communicating information lacking, but much of the relevant data are classified. To state and local officials, however, the classification problems often look like a smoke screen obscuring a mindset on the part of federal officials that the war on terrorism is primarily a federal responsibility.

September 11 and the investigations in its wake laid bare the nation's deficiencies in intelligence.[2] U.S. intelligence had produced a reasonably substantive understanding of al Qaeda and its network. It had detected indications of impending attacks, in the United States as elsewhere, as those signals became increasingly shrill over the summer of 2001. However, the nation's ability to follow the specific trail of hijackers in and out of the country and to "connect the dots" of specific threats at home foundered on the ragged sharing of information between intelligence and law enforcement. Another shortcoming arose from the way that the FBI conceived its mission, which primarily centered on after-the-fact criminal investigations rather than prevention of terrorism and other crimes.

Whether the government could have done enough with the information it had to avert the attacks will remain one of history's enduring puzzles. Probably the answer is no. Recent books, like that by senior counterterrorism officer Richard Clarke, reveal more details, and the blue-ribbon panel investigating September 11 will reveal still more. The picture that emerges is of a shriller and shriller warning over the summer of 2001 of an impending al Qaeda attack.[3] That warning seems to have still been general. Yet, had the pieces that were available been put together and the leads pursued, the government would have known that suspected terrorists were in the country and might have located them; airlines and others would have been notified to look out for other dangerous individuals; flying lessons would have come under scrutiny. To be sure, taking flying lessons is not a crime, not even if the students are Arabs and the lessons do not include takeoffs and landings. So it is not obvious what the government would have done with that information. But greater concern about unusual activity at flight schools might have heightened searches at airports and in other ways disrupted al Qaeda's efforts enough to cause the terrorists to change or defer their plans.

This chapter reviews what has happened—or has not happened—at the DHS. It then steps back to look at the roots of the September 11 failure, the sources of the problems that remain, and what is required from intelligence for the security of the nation. So far, intelligence, like other government specialist agencies responding to September 11, has resembled children's soccer, with everyone running to the ball, in this case the ball called counterterrorism. The DHS plainly has a role to play in intelligence, especially with its Information Analysis and Infrastructure Protection Directorate, but so do other agencies. All of the innovations to date, in intelligence and beyond, represent compromises among competing interests. No structure is ever ideal. The right perspective is to keep focused on what the nation needs and wait to see whether the innovations made can be effective.

THE DHS AND INTELLIGENCE

The DHS established the Information Analysis Infrastructure Protection (IAIP) Directorate, headed by an undersecretary and two assistant secretaries, one directly responsible for information analysis and the other for infrastructure protection. Not surprisingly, the DHS has concentrated on beginning to knit together its twenty-two far-flung components, especially in the realm of information technology. The roles, missions, and functions of each assistant secretary's portfolio are still very much evolving, although it is possible to describe their general contours. On the information-sharing side, the DHS has been criticized for being slow off the mark. According to the Markle Foundation task force:

> DHS . . . does not appear to have taken the necessary steps to build the communications and sharing network required to deal with the threat, or to begin producing regular, actionable intelligence products for other agencies. Indeed, the DHS has yet to articulate a vision of how it will link federal, state, and local agencies in a communications and sharing network, or what its role will be with respect to the TTIC and other federal agencies. . . . Moreover, neither the TTIC nor the DHS has gotten very far in putting in place the necessary staff or framework for analyzing information and sharing it broadly among the relevant federal, state, and local agencies. Government at the federal level thus remains very much in need of an overarching decentralized framework for building an information sharing and analysis network.[4]

Logically, the IAIP should be the transmission belt between the intelligence community, which produces threat information, and non-federal officials responsible for defending potential targets. So far, threat information has been in short supply, especially for state and local officials. As a result, the nation has not really undergone a threat assessment. Instead, it has focused on *vulnerability* assessment. Because any democracy's vulnerabilities are legion, the consequence of highlighting them has been mostly to frighten citizens and local authorities. But if threat assessments become better and more regular, the IAIP and the DHS could translate the information provided by the intelligence community into a form useful to local public safety officials.

On the analysis side, the IAIP collates and assesses data from multiple sources—including the FBI, the CIA, the National Security Agency, the Drug Enforcement Administration, the Energy Department, the Customs Service, and the Transportation Department—and acts as a clearinghouse for all information relevant to homeland security and related critical infrastructure protection threats. Although it has no specific collection powers of its own, the IAIP has a mandate to act as a repository for "raw" intelligence from both the FBI and the CIA. Over time, it will be able to "task" those agencies and other intelligence collectors with data-gathering assignments that serve its own priorities and agenda.

Getting the IAIP up and running has been chaotic. The first assistant secretary for information analysis left after only a few months on the job, and it took four months to find his replacement. Meanwhile, the small number of analysts in that office have been running hard to carve out their role and answer questions from infrastructure managers as well as state and local officials.

Given the IAIP's slow start, it is perhaps no bad thing that the TTIC took much of the broader "connect the dots" role from the DHS. A handful of DHS analysts do participate directly in the TTIC's work, and the IAIP receives and analyzes terrorism-related information from the TTIC and other intelligence agencies to: (1) map threats against existing vulnerability assessments, (2) recommend responses to identified challenges and contingencies, and (3) set national priorities for critical infrastructure protection. The directorate is meant to act as the main intelligence conduit for the federal government, ensuring that threat assessments generated by the TTIC are disseminated quickly to the public, private industry, and state and local government and law enforcement officials.[5]

What the DHS "publishes" so far mostly derives from its inheritance of the National Infrastructure Protection Center, formerly part of the FBI. The DHS produces infrastructure warnings under the titles of assessments, advisories, alerts, and information bulletins (InfoBulletins), which are developed and distributed through its advisory and information-sharing system.[6] Many of these briefings naturally contain classified information, but the DHS, like other agencies, is working to find ways to strip out sensitive material so that it can be distributed widely. Those who could benefit from that intelligence include the information sharing and analysis centers

(ISACs) that exist for critical, national infrastructures—such as finance, telecommunications, transport, power distribution, and air traffic control—law enforcement authorities, including at the state and local level, and private citizens who manage parts of those infrastructures or other critical facilities, like nuclear power plants or ports.

For the DHS and the IAIP, both logic and the established work of other agencies point toward keeping information analysis tightly linked to infrastructure protection. That would mean leaving it to other agencies to write perceptive papers on long-term trends in al Qaeda funding. Rather, DHS's intelligence role would be, in Paul Redmond's language, a "Noah's ark" of tactical analysis, oriented domestically toward the networks and nerve centers that the DHS is charged with protecting. It would have a cadre of analysts numbering in the low three figures recruited from several sources, including the military and police. Given the distinctions between intelligence and law enforcement, however, finding the right police officers to retrain for domestic intelligence work requires careful selection.

Another source of intelligence analysts would be the facilities at risk themselves, some of which already had created information-sharing and analysis centers. Indeed, some are even more organized. The nation's railroads, for instance, have a warning system of their own, complete with scrambler telephones for conducting conversations in confidence. The private sector also has its information analysts. The Southern Poverty Law Center, for instance, has for years kept careful databases on domestic militias and other hate groups.

The virtue of the DHS is that its components—eighteen thousand agents in customs and border protection, fifteen thousand employees in citizenship and immigration services, and forty-eight thousand screeners in transportation security—are all potential intelligence collectors. The word "collection" remains taboo because the DHS does not have a mandate to gather intelligence. But its capacity to do so is significant.

As for the FBI, the challenge is to alter its culture so that when customs agents discern something that is anomalous or otherwise may be of interest to someone else, they pass the information along even if it is not immediately relevant to their work.

THE ROOTS OF FAILURE

Turf battles and inertia surely played a role in allowing the attacks of September 11 to happen, but the roots of failure were structural and trace back to arrangements that had served the nation well during the cold war. It was not surprising that cooperation between the CIA and the FBI before September 11 was ragged at best. We wanted it that way. Out of concern for our civil liberties, the nation decided the two agencies should not be too close. The FBI and the CIA sat astride the fundamental distinctions of the cold war—distinctions between intelligence and law enforcement, between foreign and domestic, and between public and private.

Law enforcement and intelligence are very different worlds, with different missions, operating codes, and standards.[7] Intelligence is oriented toward the future and toward policy—that is, it seeks to inform the making of policy. Contending with a blizzard of uncertainty where the "truth" will never be precisely located, intelligence seeks to interpret new information in light of its existing understanding of complex situations. Thus, its standard is likely to be "good enough to serve as a basis for policy." Because intelligence strives above all to protect sources and methods, its officials want desperately to stay out of the chain of evidence so they will not have to testify in court.

By contrast, law enforcement is oriented toward response. Its business is not policy but prosecution, and its method is cases. It strives to put bad guys in jail. Its standard is high: "good enough for a court of law." And law enforcement knows that, if it is to make a case, it must be prepared to reveal something about how it knows what it knows; at least it is aware that it will face that possibility. It has no real history of conducting analysis; indeed, the meaning of the word "intelligence" is different for law enforcement—it means "tips" to help find and convict evildoers more than looking for patterns of behavior to frame future policy decisions. Law enforcement and policing also traditionally have been defined in terms of geographic units. These definitions are more and more mismatched to threats, like terrorism, that respect no geographic boundaries.

Another distinction, between foreign versus domestic, magnifies the intelligence/law enforcement disconnect. American institutions and practices both during and prior to the cold war drew a sharp barrier between home and abroad. The FBI had conducted wartime espionage and counterespionage in Latin America, and in December 1944, J. Edgar Hoover had proposed that the FBI run worldwide intelligence operations along the lines of those Latin American operations.[8] The proposal had some support outside the FBI, at the State Department in particular. But President Harry Truman worried openly that giving the intelligence mandate to the FBI would risk creating a "Gestapo-like" organization, and so foreign operations went first to the Central Intelligence Group, CIA's predecessor, and then to the CIA. Both, however, were barred from law enforcement and domestic operations, a prohibition that also applies to the National Security Agency.

One more distinction is public versus private. During the cold war, national security was a federal government monopoly. To be sure, private companies and citizens played a role, but for most citizens, fighting the cold war simply meant paying their taxes. That is not so for the campaign against terrorism and for homeland security. Civilians' lives will be affected—ranging from the inconvenience of waiting in long lines at airports to harder questions about how much security efforts will rely on national data banks and the controversy over biometrics (biological identifiers such as fingerprints or retinal scans). Across the country, there are three times as many "police" in the private sector as in governments.

These distinctions were not imposed by nature. Rather, the United States mostly chose them for good, practical, and constitutional reasons. They did not serve us badly during the cold war, but they set us up to fail in an era of terror. Their shortcomings were all too vividly on display before September 11, for instance in the ragged relations between the FBI and the CIA, and the relatively low priority the FBI accorded to terrorism.[9] Now, reshaping intelligence and law enforcement means not just reshuffling organizations and refashioning their cultures; it means rethinking basic categories of threat and response.

Much discussion of "domestic intelligence" or "homeland security" intelligence lacks clarity, so it is worth contemplating what the nation needs, as demonstrated by September 11. Those needs run from intelligence analysis to intelligence support for operations to collecting useful information effectively. Analytically, the principal requirement is to do a better job of "connecting the dots" of information from abroad and at home to produce much more sophisticated assessments of the terrorist threat, especially on American soil, to communications, electric power, and transport.

Operationally, the nation needs:

♦ Better communication, especially between the CIA and the FBI, in following leads, suspicious people, or activities inside and outside the United States;

♦ Ways to give state and local law enforcement officials, in particular, some guidance about what to be on the lookout for in doing their daily business and some means of getting the information they collect into a form that can be shared and analyzed;

♦ Much more common standards for assembling and sharing "watch lists" across the range of agencies—including non-"intelligence" agencies such as the State Department or the Federal Aviation Administration.

In terms of collection, the questions are whether there are enough "dots" of information collected at home and how more might be gathered effectively without trampling on the rights of innocent citizens and others. The needs might be expressed as:

♦ Giving federal officials, especially FBI agents, more tools and somewhat more latitude in collecting information relevant to the war on terrorism, including data collected outside the confines of an ongoing criminal case.

♦ Finding ways to make a wide range of federal officials—in the DHS especially—as well as state and local law enforcement officers "embedded collectors" of information in the war on terrorism.

BETTER DOT CONNECTING

This is the task of assembling information to understand the nature of the terrorist threat, especially to the homeland, and several initiatives are under way. The most notable has been the TTIC. But the FBI has moved in parallel to do better threat assessment. Created in May 2003, TTIC reports to the director of central intelligence. Its mandate is precisely to connect the dots, minimizing the seams in the analysis of counterterrorism intelligence collected overseas and within the United States. In that sense, the executive branch assigned to the TTIC many of the analytic functions that Congress—and many outsiders (including this author)—had recommended be the job of the DHS's Information Analysis and Infrastructure Protection Directorate.[10] The TTIC incorporates elements from the FBI's Counterterrorism Division and the CIA's Counterterrorist Center,[11] and it also includes representatives from the DHS, the Justice Department, the State Department, and the Department of Defense. The TTIC is scheduled to move out of CIA headquarters next year and into its own building, in northern Virginia not far from the CIA. This will create a powerful counterterrorism federation: three hundred people from the TTIC, plus six hundred to eight hundred from central intelligence's Counterterrorist Center and five hundred to six hundred from the FBI Counterterrorism Division.

The TTIC's mandate is to perform the following tasks:

♦ Conduct threat analysis and inform overall collection strategies, though, like DHS, it will have no authorization to collect information on its own;

♦ Create a structure to institutionalize the sharing of all terrorist intelligence across agency lines to generate the most detailed and informed threat picture possible;

♦ Provide ongoing and comprehensive assessments to the national leadership;

♦ Develop a system to identify the nation's intelligence requirements in the war on terrorism, and to task the intelligence collectors to meet those requirements;

♦ Maintain an up-to-date database of known and suspected terrorists and ensure that it is made available to appropriate officials at all levels of government.[12]

Some of the obstacles the TTIC confronts in carrying out its mandate, such as the very different cultures of intelligence and law enforcement, are long-standing, but surmounting them is far more imperative in the post–September 11 era. Others, such as acquiring new sources of domestic intelligence from state and local officials and effectively sharing intelligence throughout this broader community, are brand new. New ways of operating, new channels of communication, and new procedures for sharing classified information will be needed.

Insiders admit that the TTIC may not be the ultimate answer, but it is beginning to function. And it is fostering more cooperation among agencies, especially between the CIA and the FBI. The TTIC was intended to be established in phases and so far has concentrated on its "connecting the dots" analytic function, in particular producing the President's Terrorism Threat Report. It is not the only agency doing such work. NORTHCOM, the newly established military command for the homeland, does something similar, and the Defense Intelligence Agency's Joint Task Force for Combating Terrorism also is "running to the soccer ball." The CIA also includes items on terrorism in its President's Daily Brief.

One immediate concern about the TTIC is that it, like virtually every other intelligence institution, is overwhelmed with current reporting. As a result, neither it nor any other unit has much time for deeper inquiries into, for instance, the links between terrorist groups and state-sponsored weapons of mass destruction programs, let alone work on evolving terrorist threats.

A longer-run concern is that the TTIC's origins in foreign intelligence will hamper its efforts to work with domestic agencies.[13] The CIA's Counterterrorist Center, which includes representatives of fifteen agencies,[14] was created in 1986 to facilitate interagency cooperation in the collection of intelligence on international terrorist groups and nation-state sponsors. It had an overseas as well as an operational orientation, so reshaping it as part of the TTIC to work across foreign and domestic lines will require a change in culture and may run up against legal issues connected with the limits of the director of central intelligence's mandate.

Those limitations remain the basis for the argument that the "connect the dots" intelligence operation ought to be lodged in the DHS. The statute setting up the DHS does call for the secretary to "access, receive, and analyze law enforcement information, intelligence information, and other information" from all levels of government and the private sector and to "integrate such information" to detect and identify threats of terrorism against the U.S. homeland.[15] The questions about lodging the analysis function in the DHS are the obverse of those pertaining to the TTIC: would it, with a primarily domestic orientation, be able to track the foreign roots of a threat, and would it, as an untried newcomer, be able to get access to all the information it needed? In any case, the Bush administration took another course in establishing the TTIC. For now, the best perspective is to keep focused on the need, not the instrument, and to give the new entity time to see if it can develop effectively.

At the same time, the FBI has been seeking to upgrade its intelligence. The bureau's own internal audits long have recognized shortcomings in its strategic intelligence capabilities. Those audits noted that the agency lacked sufficient quantities of high-level analysts, with most having little or no training in intelligence assessment procedures and devoid of either academic or professional experience in the subject matter for which they were responsible. A May 2000 Justice Department report also found that the FBI lacked a viable information management system to correlate and integrate extrapolated field intelligence.[16]

To change this state of affairs, the bureau created, in December 2001, an Office of Intelligence, which was to support both counterterrorism and, more generically, counterintelligence. It is supposed to focus on improving the bureau's ability to collect, consolidate, assess, and disseminate information on vital national security matters. The office will also oversee the development of a College of Analytical Studies, which will train FBI recruits in the latest intelligence assessment and forecasting procedures and is designed to lay the foundation for a dedicated analyst career track that would be of interest to those not normally attracted to a future in law enforcement.[17]

Subsequently, FBI director Robert Mueller reorganized the top of his agency, creating four executive assistant directors, including one for intelligence, charged first and foremost with counterterrorism but ranging across the bureau's missions. The creation of that office signals the upgrading of intelligence in an organizational culture dominated by special agents, one in which all others, including analysts, were relegated to the label "support." The Office of Intelligence now contributes to the President's Terrorism Threat Report. Mueller and CIA director George Tenet often meet with the president jointly, delivering both the FBI materials and the CIA-prepared President's Daily Brief.

IMPROVING OPERATIONS: "SHARING THE DOTS"

Connecting the dots is the analytic task of putting together what information is available. "Sharing the dots" is the operational challenge of making sure that information moves to those who need it. Here, too, September 11 provided a powerful impetus to change. Before the attacks, very different cultures deepened the wall between intelligence and law enforcement.[18] For instance, FBI agents have top secret clearances, but few are cleared into the special compartmentalized information that is the woof and warp of intelligence.[19] So, when faced with unfamiliar FBI counterparts in meetings, CIA officers might be uncertain about how much they could say. FBI agents, in turn, feared that inadvertent disclosures might jeopardize prosecutions. The safest course was to say nothing. If the conversation turned to domestic matters, then the CIA officials would also be uncertain how much they should hear.

After the attacks, officials who were formerly reluctant to share information began doing so. Conversations that did not happen before the attacks began to take place. Postmortems of major surprises, like the joint congressional inquiry into September 11, usually conclude that what was lacking was attention and money. The response to September 11 has provided plenty of both.

Major changes have occurred at the FBI in the months since the September 11 attacks, structurally, functionally, and operationally, and the transformation continues apace. These changes bear on intelligence, though indirectly. By tradition, the FBI's organizational culture was not just agent dominated but also very decentralized, with the bureau's fifty-six field offices having considerable autonomy. That was especially true for the three biggest offices, in Washington, New York, and Los Angeles. Moreover, the bureau was—and still is—preeminently an investigative law enforcement institution, not an intelligence organization. Its special agents naturally were attracted to where there were "collars"—that is, arrests—to be made. Terrorism work offered less attraction, for terrorists ultimately might commit but one crime. Accordingly, the FBI viewed the world through the lens of the case and case file. If information was not relevant to making a case, it was not of much account.

Now Mueller has made counterterrorism the bureau's number-one priority, and there has been a major overhaul and expansion of the FBI's Counterterrorism Division, which will take the lead in all terrorism-related cases from the field offices. Integral to this reorganization has been the transfer of counterterrorism personnel to central headquarters in Washington, along with shifting other agents from criminal and drug work to the antiterrorism mission. To give it added force, specialized "flying squads" are being set up to coordinate national counterterrorism investigations and augment local field capabilities. These units can be sent out quickly and are intended to respond rapidly and resolve unfolding contingencies, particularly in areas where the FBI has little or no presence.[20]

The idea is to centralize operations and thereby facilitate communication across field offices. Expertise will be concentrated at a single location rather than dispersed and thereby diluted across multiple jurisdictions. Moreover, transferred agents will be encouraged and rewarded for remaining in counterterrorism work for an extended period of time, both to develop their personal skills and to deepen cooperative working relationships. This concentration on counterterrorism is a notable departure from the FBI's traditional procedure of regularly rotating agents through a variety of assignments. Agents who wanted promotions knew that spending time on criminal work was critical to their success.

Addressing shortcomings in the FBI's famously backward technological capacities is critical to both operations and intelligence. Given a choice between more agents on the street or better technology, the bureau in the past opted for the former. So the FBI was, in the words of one investigator, "where the [IBM] 360s went to die." Or, as an FBI agent put it to me, "We took the dirt road alternative to the information superhighway a generation ago."[21]

Now, a half-billion-dollar, multiphased process known as Trilogy is in motion, though it has been dogged by problems. It is intended to upgrade the bureau's capacity to collect, store, search, retrieve, assess, and disseminate data, and by January 2004, it was meant to provide all bureau field sites with improved network communications, a common and current set of office automation tools, and user-friendly Web site applications.[22] A three-step information technology infrastructure enhancement strategy also has been planned. Ultimately, this will allow classified data to be shared internally among FBI analysts and disseminated among the wider intelligence community.

A new National Joint Terrorism Task Force has been established, which will be equipped with a constantly updated counterterrorism watch list and document exploitation and communications analysis centers. The National Joint Terrorism Task Force will coordinate the existing pool of city-level joint terrorism task forces, which now number eighty-four and counting, as well as six ad hoc regional terrorism task forces that are already in place across the country.[23]

Information and intelligence now flows more freely among the federal agencies, especially the FBI and CIA—in the TTIC, the joint terrorism task forces, and elsewhere. Yet the harder challenge remains sharing across federal, state, and local jurisdictions, not to mention deciding what should be divulged to private citizens. It is fair to say that all the agencies have concentrated on their immediate tasks—for the TTIC and the DHS that meant getting themselves up and running, and for the FBI it meant moving forward with the change in its mission. Sharing with state and local authorities has taken a back seat.

Moreover, such sharing as is occurring is thus far a one-way street, from federal to state and local. There are not as yet processes to give state and local authorities guidance about what to look for, or to collect and analyze what they discover. The TTIC has begun to design a system for sharing information between the FBI and the DHS. The TTIC has created "TTIC Online," which operates at the special compartmentalized information classification level and now reaches some twenty-five hundred users, almost entirely in the federal government. It plans to create a secret-level classification version, stripping the sources from information where necessary, and then a version at the "sensitive but unclassified" level, which could be much more easily shared with state and local authorities.

The FBI's primary vehicle for sharing information with state and local law enforcement officials is the joint terrorism task forces, which have mushroomed in number and play an important role. Yet, the FBI dominates the joint terrorism task forces. For example, because the internal FBI network is top secret, state and local officials must be cleared to that level in order to participate in the task forces—a process that can be slow and one that many local police chiefs find galling.

The DHS was assigned the responsibility for coordinating information sharing with authorities beyond the federal level. A recent General Accounting Office study, however, found no level of authority very satisfied with the sharing process. In the survey, only 13 percent of the federal officials and 35 percent of state officials found sharing between the two "effective" or "very effective."[24] Of the big cities surveyed, 98 percent reported that they needed information on the movement of known terrorists, but only 15 percent said they received it. The same obstacle is reported over and over: federal officials regard the war on terrorism as primarily a federal responsibility, and they express concern about sharing intelligence with state and local authorities.

Moreover, the problem of trust is compounded by the lack of an infrastructure for sharing information. The information technology systems of many police departments make the FBI's look pretty good.[25] Gilman Louie, president of In-Q-Tel, the CIA's high-tech venture capital company, likens the need to having a "soda straw" reaching from intelligence agencies down to the cop on the beat. Now, however, there is effectively no straw. Nor is there policy and guidance to govern what should flow through the straw in either direction, either guidance to the cop about what to look for or information from him or her that might be analyzed in the context of other information.

On the watch-list issue, too, there is a long way to go after some modest progress. Nine federal agencies—including the FBI, the Bureau of Immigration and Customs Enforcement, the DHS, the Pentagon, and the State Department—maintain lists to spot terrorist suspects trying to get a visa, board a plane, or cross a border. A new Terrorist Screening Center is supposed to consolidate the existing watch lists.[26] The TTIC is creating a Terrorist Identity Data Mark, assembling Counterterrorist Center and State Department "TIPOFF" watch-lists. However, in April 2003, the General Accounting Office criticized the various agencies for not sharing their watch-lists.

All agencies keeping such lists share information from them with other federal officials as well as local and state police officials. But the General Accounting Office study found that some agencies did not have policies for deciding when lists would be shared, and, when they did, the sharing often required complex, labor-intensive methods to cull information. Agencies typically have different types of databases and software that make sharing information next to impossible. As a result, sharing of information is often fractured: "inconsistent and limited," the study reported.[27]

Moreover, the watch-lists raise a host of civil liberties questions, and so far the government has provided little guidance to its intelligence agencies in dealing with such issues. This criticism was echoed by the Markle Foundation task force. If a "U.S. person" (citizen or resident alien) has been implicated as a suspected terrorist in an FBI investigation, he or she can be included in, say, the TTIC database. But what if the FBI investigation is only preliminary? Should there be restrictions on how widely sensitive information about the target is shared? These issues, and many others, remain to be settled.

COLLECTION: PRODUCING MORE DOTS

In the long run, more "dots" of domestic intelligence will come from state and local authorities—with local law enforcement officers and others serving as "embedded collectors," who might pass along observations made while carrying out their normal duties. So far, though, the federal authorities have sought to expand the gathering of dots in just two ways, neither of which yet involve the DHS. The USA Patriot Act of November 2001 loosened the ground rules for searches and wiretaps under the Foreign Intelligence and Surveillance Act (FISA), which enables a court operating in secret to grant covert wiretap and other surveillance authority for intelligence—as opposed to law enforcement—purposes. And the guidelines under which FBI agents operate have been loosened.

The case of Zacarias Moussaoui spurred action to ease restrictions on the Foreign Intelligence and Surveillance Act. Moussaoui, accused of being the so-called twentieth hijacker, was arrested on August 16, 2001, in Minneapolis for a visa violation. FBI agents at the field office suspected him of terrorism and sought, with increasing desperation, to search his laptop computer but were denied permission by FBI headquarters. Before September 11, obtaining foreign intelligence information had to be the purpose of FISA surveillance.[28] If evidence of crime were uncovered in the course of the wiretap, that evidence was admissible in court—but the foreign intelligence purpose was paramount. The Patriot Act loosened the requirement to "a significant purpose."[29]

The specter of COINTELPRO more than a generation ago hangs over all these efforts to generate more dots. COINTELPRO was a pernicious mixing of intelligence, or counterintelligence, and law enforcement at the FBI. The ostensible justification for these "counterintelligence programs" was to combat the operations of hostile foreign intelligence services.[30] But most of COINTELPRO's specific targets were American citizens involved in civil rights and antiwar groups. People like Martin Luther King, Jr., were not only watched but harassed and worse. Because FISA wiretaps do not require probable cause of a crime and are longer, more flexible, and less controlled by judges than are those for law enforcement taps, there is concern that the broader surveillance authority will be used to troll for the purposes of law enforcement. This led to tensions between the FBI and the Federal Intelligence and Surveillance Court over who can approve the sharing of FISA data with FBI law enforcement agents.

In November 2002, a federal court ruling upheld more sharing of intelligence across the intelligence/law enforcement divide within the FBI, and in October 2003, new guidelines went to the field offices confirming the change.[31] Before the Patriot Act, the bureau would have had to open separate wiretaps—a criminal one based on a court order and a FISA one for intelligence purposes—and would have been sharply constrained in sharing information between the two. Under the new guidelines, it could open a single FISA surveillance probe looking, for example, both at whether a suspect was part of a terrorist organization and whether he or she planned to buy explosives. Agents working on the two aspects of the case could now cooperate closely.

Concerns over civil liberties also arose in the second of the federal initiatives to produce more dots. FBI leadership began a series of functional changes designed to make the bureau more proactive. The thrust of these reforms has relaxed old rules restricting the monitoring of religious institutions, political organizations, and individual suspects without first establishing probable cause that they were involved in criminal activity. In addition, prohibitions barring special agents from attending public gatherings or pursuing terrorist leads in generic databases and on the Internet have largely been scrapped.[32] In one sense, agents only are being permitted to do what other citizens can do; at the same time, they are agents, not ordinary citizens.

These issues about how to recalibrate the balance between security and liberty in collecting domestic intelligence are fundamental for American democracy, and they can be resolved only over time. So, too, the institutional distinctions that were reinforced by the lessons learned during the cold war era should be altered with care. Only with experience will the roles of the various agencies be sorted out, in intelligence as in other areas of homeland security. Meanwhile, the spectacle of everyone "running to the ball" is messy and inefficient.

Still, it is better that they *are* running rather than standing still. For the DHS, the challenge remains to get into the game effectively and decisively.

3.

IMMIGRATION

T. Alexander Aleinikoff

Before September 11, 2001, both the Clinton and Bush administrations had developed plans to reorganize immigration activities within the executive branch. The 1997 report of the U.S. Commission on Immigration Reform (the "Jordan Commission") had called for dismantling the Immigration and Naturalization Service (INS) and placing its components in other federal departments.[1] Legislation introduced in Congress would have folded the immigration apparatus more fully into the Department of Justice, creating separate bureaus (akin to the FBI) for the service functions (processing of applications for immigrant status, work authorization, asylum, and naturalization) and law enforcement functions (border patrol, detention and removal of noncitizens unlawfully in the United States, and investigation of smuggling and unauthorized employment of noncitizens).[2] The Clinton administration's plan was more modest: abolish the INS district offices and establish separate service and enforcement chains of command within the INS. Outside experts suggested more radical plans, such as the establishment of a new freestanding immigration agency within the executive branch.[3]

All of these proposals were based on the recognition that the INS was a troubled agency. Underfunded and inadequately managed for years, the agency accomplished neither its service nor enforcement missions well. Millions waited for their applications for status to be processed and resolved; millions of undocumented migrants resided within the United States with little likelihood of being apprehended or removed. The Clinton administration devoted significant new funds to border enforcement (more than doubling the size of the Border Patrol), but it could point to no credible evidence that the added resources had in fact deterred illegal entry into the United States. The INS also struggled under the burden of major legislative initiatives in 1990 and 1996 that required new programs, regulations, and substantial retraining of personnel.

The events of September 11 put new emphasis on reorganization. The hijackers were noncitizens who had entered through lawful immigration channels (although subsequent investigation has found that some were improperly granted visas). The straw that broke the camel's back was the arrival of immigration documents at a Venice, Florida, flight school for two of the hijackers six months after they had flown planes into the Twin Towers. The event was widely misreported: the documents were not visas but rather copies of visas approved in July and August 2001 that had been retained by INS contractors and mailed as a matter of routine to the flight school. But the damage was done. President Bush showed anger at a press conference a day after the news broke. Stating that he was "stunned and not happy," he continued: "Look, the INS needs to be reformed. And it's one of the reasons why I have called for the separation of the paperwork side of the INS from the enforcement side. And obviously the paperwork side needs a lot of work. It's inexcusable." As plans proceeded with the new Department of Homeland Security (DHS), the Bush administration announced its intention that all INS functions be transferred there.

Some members of Congress had other ideas, arguing that only the enforcement side of the INS should go to the Department of Homeland Security. The service functions could stay at the Department of Justice or go to the State Department. Ultimately the administration prevailed, but the battle resulted in a peculiar arrangement within the DHS. The Homeland Security Act placed the enforcement function under the DHS Directorate for Border and Transportation Safety. Headed by an undersecretary, the directorate also took over the functions of the Customs Service, agricultural inspections, the Transportation Security Agency, and the Federal Protective Service. Because there was no obvious place for the INS's service functions in the enforcement-minded new department, they were placed in a DHS Bureau of Citizenship and Immigration Services (now known as USCIS), reporting directly to the deputy secretary.

The Bush administration brought the Homeland Security Act into force on March 1, 2003, officially abolishing the INS as of that date. The statute would have permitted a transition date as late as January 2004. Curiously, the March 1 date preceded by three months the time frame set by Congress for providing a detailed implementation plan for the immigration reorganization.[4] Under authority granted by the statute, the Bush administration rearranged the Directorate for Border and Transportation Safety. The Homeland Security Act had placed all immigration enforcement activities in one bureau. The president's reorganization adopted a more functional approach. It established a Bureau of Customs and Border Protection—which included the Border Patrol, immigration inspectors, agricultural inspectors, and customs border inspectors—and a Bureau of Immigration and Customs Enforcement (dubbed "ICE"), which combined immigration and customs investigators focused on law enforcement in the interior and the Federal Protective Service. This complicated arrangement is shown in the Appendix, page 96, which clearly illustrates the potential structural obstacles to effective coordination of immigration functions within the DHS.

PROMISES MADE

The original impetus for reorganization at the INS was to improve performance by separating units that deal with immigration, naturalization, and asylum applications from law enforcement units. For years, these had been combined in thirty-three district offices around the country, and the poor results were obvious to all. The statute creating the DHS required reports from both units detailing how they planned to improve their performance.[5] Congress mandated that the DHS "reduce the backlog in the processing of immigration benefit applications, with the objective of the total elimination of the backlog one year" after the date of enactment of the Homeland Security Act.[6] And, once up and running, the new department affirmed a goal announced by President Bush in July 2001, at a ceremony on Ellis Island, of a "six-month standard from start to finish" for processing immigration applications.

Just a year later, it is too early to judge fully the success or failure in meeting these goals. Reorganization on the scale mandated by the legislation—involving not just a division of INS functions but also merging them with customs and agricultural inspection—is a difficult undertaking. But a preliminary assessment based on extensive interviews with officials in the DHS and others is that the results have been mixed. While progress has been made on some fronts, structural and cultural factors will continue to impede effective performance of immigration agencies for some time to come.

PERFORMANCE

IMMIGRATION SERVICES

According to U.S. Citizenship and Immigration Services (USCIS) director Eduardo Aguirre, the bureau has established three overriding priorities: reducing processing time for all benefits applications to six months, improving customer service, and enhancing national security.

BACKLOG REDUCTION. Backlogs have substantially increased, rather than declined, over the past year. In March 2003, USCIS faced a backlog of about 5.2 million pending immigration applications. As of October 31, 2003, the number was more than 5.4 million. The number of pending naturalization applications remained virtually unchanged (more than six hundred thousand), despite a 25 percent decrease in filings for FY 2003.[7]

The number of pending cases is not necessarily a measure of delay. That is, with enough personnel or a reengineered application process, even a heavy caseload could be decided speedily. But resources for this work have not increased at USCIS, nor has the application process been made significantly more efficient. Thus, the number of pending cases translates into exceptionally long waits for applicants. For example, there are more than 1.2 million applications for green cards in the backlog. Ripple effects include delays in the eligibility of individuals for naturalization and their ability to bring family members to the United States.

The immigration reform proposal announced by President Bush on January 7, 2004, would only serve to worsen the existing backlogs and delays. Under the plan, employers could file applications for a legal temporary status for their undocumented workers. The numbers are potentially huge—there are perhaps as many as 8 million undocumented immigrants in the United States today.

The administration's budget for fiscal year 2005 proposes a $60 million increase for backlog-reduction efforts. In addition, the DHS has recently proposed increases in fees charged to applicants for immigration benefits. This is projected to net an additional $150 million, which would be applied to the resolution of immigration and naturalization cases. It remains to be seen whether these proposals will actually yield new resources and how quickly such resources can be translated into hiring and training new personnel.

There are several reasons for the growing backlogs. Any reorganization plan entails initial delays as new channels of authority are established, personnel are reassigned (or positions go unfilled), and support services are reorganized. But far more important appears to be the continuing impact of September 11, in three respects.

First, all benefits applications are subject to multiple security checks—through the FBI, CIA, State Department, and other government databases. These searches are neither fully automatic nor coordinated. Frequently they will produce "hits"—based, for example, on a name match or prior immigration violation—that require additional researching of files. Because of variations in spellings, particularly with the discrepancies in the transliteration of Arabic names, investigators searching databases must be alert to possible misspellings. Furthermore, it was discovered after September 11 that the FBI checks relied on by the INS were incomplete and inaccurate because they had been run through only one of the bureau's databases—based on individuals' names—and not another that collected information based on investigations of companies.[8] Because of the obvious security defects of that process, the INS then decided to run all pending applications—more than 3.2 million—through another FBI check. The administration made no public announcement of the problem or the delays caused by the solution. (Apparently, no plans exist for subjecting previously approved applications to the new, full FBI screening.) The new security measures will improve the applications process. But until fully automated and integrated systems can be put in place, these measures will inevitably slow down application processing.

Second, the post–September 11 culture among immigration officials has clearly favored denials of applications where any doubt at all exists. After the flight school incident, INS commissioner James Ziglar issued a "zero tolerance" order. The memorandum lectured INS employees that "disregarding field guidance or other INS policy will not be tolerated. The days of looking the other way are over. . . . Individuals who fail to abide by issued field guidance or other INS policy will be disciplined appropriately." The memo seems unobjectionable; it simply asks employees to do what is already required of them. But in field offices, the memo generated great concern because INS policy guidance had not been effectively organized and disseminated. Thus, officials feared that they would be held responsible for violating policies of which they were unaware. This produced an attitude of better safe than sorry: better to deny an application than violate some policy in approving it.

According to immigration attorneys around the nation, there has been a dramatic increase in denials and requests for additional information in routine business and family visa applications. Indeed, attorneys have a phrase for this development: "the culture of no." Ziglar's "zero tolerance" order was rescinded in late 2003 by Aguirre, who stated that other measures have been put in place to make the application process more secure; officials now are being asked to rely on their expertise and to exercise judgment, instead of routinely denying cases in which there is even the slightest question about eligibility. But it is not clear that this shift has had an impact among the decisionmakers.

Third, immigration officials were tapped to implement the "call-in" registration program of the newly minted National Security Entry-Exit Registration System (NSEERS). Under this program, males from specified countries (all but one of them predominantly Muslim or Arab nations) holding nonimmigrant visas were required to report to local DHS offices to be fingerprinted, photographed, and interviewed. Approximately 83,500 people were registered under the program. In December 2003, the DHS eased rules requiring registrants to come back to DHS offices a year later, and no new call-ins are planned. This has permitted USCIS officials to return to their normal tasks.

USCIS intends to roll out a comprehensive backlog reduction plan in the spring of 2004. According to a January 6 fact sheet, the plan will focus on producing immigration documents more efficiently, streamlining the process for some family and business visas, as well as naturalization and work authorization requests, and eliminating requirements that contribute to delays (for example, by lengthening the time that certain documents are valid in order to cut down on renewal applications).

CUSTOMER SERVICE. USCIS has implemented first steps toward improved customer service. The bureau now permits electronic filing of several applications (such as work authorization and green card replacement and renewal). In the future, perhaps 90 percent of all immigration applications will be filed electronically. The Miami district office has piloted a program that permits people to schedule meetings electronically with USCIS personnel. Measures such as these can reduce time spent waiting in lines at USCIS local offices. (Of course, policies that make filing applications easier also may have the effect of adding to the backlog of pending cases.) Other offices have reduced lines by reconfiguring waiting rooms, installing information kiosks, and notifying people of availability of forms and other information online.[9]

USCIS has created a new, toll-free customer service line that handles about one million calls per month. The bureau states that its monthly surveys show 80 percent customer satisfaction with the system, although some immigration attorneys complain the new system has caused them to lose direct access with the service centers where applications are processed and resolved.[10]

Immigration advocates and attorneys are mixed in their reviews of USCIS customer service. Some report more courteous service, fewer lost files, and better scheduling practices. Others state that little has changed at the local level and that significant inconsistencies in practice around the country, and even among bureau employees in the same office, has continued. They also express frustration at not knowing whom to contact in the new system to resolve problems.

To help improve customer service, the Homeland Security Act established an ombudsman's office within the USCIS, charged with assisting individuals and employers in resolving problems and proposing changes to practices that create difficulties.[11] The statute requires the ombudsman to appoint local ombudsmen, including at least one per state. One might think that the ombudsman and his or her staff would handle some of the huge number of inquiries directed at congressional district offices from employers, family members, and immigrants about delays in application processing, lost files, and the like.

But if that was the goal of the legislation, it is not being fulfilled: no budget has been provided for the ombudsman to open offices across the nation and to handle the large number of likely inquiries. (The 1 million calls that USCIS's customer service line receives each month gives some glimmer of the kind of workload that might face local ombudsman offices.) In practice, the office, with a small staff in the nation's capital, focuses on bigger-picture issues, such as working with the USCIS on backlog and customer service goals and policies.

Overall, it is clear that the emphasis on customer service is taken seriously at the top. In this regard, the reorganization of functions has succeeded: it has produced a cohesive program dedicated to a single mission. It also is true that security has been enhanced through revamping the application process. The difficult questions that remain are how to put in place systems that permit both efficiency and security and how to overcome the cultural after-effects of September 11 that continue to grip immigration officials. The USCIS director is confident that the president's six-month goal for application processing is attainable by 2006. But mounting backlogs and the prospect of millions of additional applications occasioned by the possibility of a new temporary worker program make that seem unlikely, particularly without substantial new resources, personnel, and the development of an effective security check system. It seems that the DHS (and perhaps the nation) has decided that lengthy processing times remain acceptable if such delays enhance security. But if the process is not improved, millions of people will continue to wait many years for naturalization and immigration benefits to which the law entitles them.

ENFORCEMENT CHALLENGES

The integration of former INS enforcement functions into the DHS has posed a more complex problem than encountered with the integration of the service functions: the INS units have been combined with bureaus from other executive branch departments. Thus, the "acculturation" process has had two elements—conceiving the immigration enforcement functions from the new DHS perspective and melding those functions with agencies that had established cultures of their own. As that process has unfolded, former INS agents have been at a disadvantage because they have traditionally been viewed in other federal enforcement departments as ineffective and poorly managed. The best evidence is the fact that the vast majority of senior supervisory positions in the field have gone to former Customs Bureau officials, not former INS agents. The morale of the latter, some say, has suffered as a result. Immigration enforcement has been hampered because customs agents, trained to investigate complex money laundering and export/import violations, are largely uninterested in arresting undocumented immigrants or fining employers who hire unauthorized workers.

On the other hand, immigration officers have generally welcomed the new opportunity to be part of agencies solely dedicated to law enforcement activities. No longer do they have to report to INS district directors who supervised both immigration services and policing at the local level. While former INS officers are now part of a bureau with broader functions—including duties relating to customs and agriculture—the mission is more sharply defined: enforce the law by detaining, prosecuting, and removing those who violate it.

Both the border and the interior enforcement bureaus are moving toward the goal of having each officer trained in all the laws enforced by his or her unit. This will, of course, take time. But it is essential for creating a more flexible and skilled enforcement effort. Immigration and Customs Enforcement (ICE) reports that its existing corps of more than seven thousand agents will be fully cross-trained by next year. Customs and Border Protection has recently graduated its first class of new agents, trained to perform immigration, customs, and agriculture duties. Plans are under way to retrain officers who worked in INS, customs, and agriculture agencies before the move to the DHS.

INTERIOR ENFORCEMENT. The Web site of ICE reports its mission as follows:

> To be the nation's preeminent law enforcement agency, dedicated to detecting vulnerabilities and preventing violations that threaten national security. Established to combat the criminal and national security threats emergent in a post 9/11 environment, ICE combines a new investigative approach with new resources to provide unparalleled investigation, interdiction,

and security services to the public and to our law enforcement partners in the federal and local sectors.[12]

Undersecretary for Border and Transportation Safety Asa Hutchinson says that combining resources under the ICE mantle has made enforcement more effective. He points to the investigation of the deaths of eighteen aliens in a smuggling operation in Texas as an example: customs' expertise in money tracing, combined with INS's skills in immigrant smuggling cases, led to the apprehension of the perpetrators.

ICE reports a number of major operations that cut across the responsibilities of its constituent parts. Examples include "Cornerstone"—aimed at identifying vulnerabilities in financial systems that permit money laundering, "Operation ICE Storm"—a multiagency initiative targeting human smuggling and smuggling-related violence in Arizona, and "Operation Predator"—directed at sexual predators, pornographers, and criminal aliens with sex offense histories.

A major focus of the DHS has been registration programs for various groups of noncitizens potentially linked with terrorism. For a number of years before September 11, INS had been pushed by Congress to tighten up the process for admitting foreign students. For years, it was well known that some students never showed up at colleges they were granted visas to attend, and other students dropped out or transferred schools without the required permission from the INS. The Student and Exchange Visitor Information System (SEVIS), brought online in early 2003, requires schools to notify the DHS electronically when students arrive and if they drop out or reduce course loads below the required minimum.

More controversial has been the National Security Entry-Exit Registration System (NSEERS), which included both a registration program at ports of entry and a call-in process for males from predominantly Muslim and Arab countries who entered the U.S. on nonimmigrant visas (that is, not as permanent resident aliens). The program was initiated by the Department of Justice in the fall of 2002 and taken over by the DHS after March 2003. More than 93,000 individuals were registered at ports of entry, and another 83,500 reported under the call-in program. Those efforts led to removal proceedings for more than 13,000 registrants owing to immigration violations. At first, the registration system required individuals registered at ports of entry to reregister thirty days later and people registered under the call-in program to reregister annually. In December 2003, the DHS rescinded the reregistration requirements, although—contrary to press reports—it did not abandon registration at ports of entry.

Policy experts who had pressed for dividing the law enforcement and service functions of INS emphasized that the separation would permit each corps of officers to do its jobs better. The idea was that each bureau would have a clearer understanding of its purposes and goals and would be guided by a clear chain of command. On the enforcement side, this appears to be happening, but it raises the question of what it means to do one's job "better." What seems to have been lost in the separation of functions is a sense of balance promoted by the combination of tasks within a single agency. At the INS, there was some truth to the claim that the law enforcement presence made those working on the services side more knowledgeable about issues related to fraud and illegality; conversely, the services side helped the investigators and enforcers understand the importance of prosecutorial discretion and flexibility with respect to claims involving humanitarian concerns. That kind of synergy appears to have lessened considerably. The officers in the Bureau of Immigration and Customs Enforcement seemed pleased with the hard-edged acronym ICE, which is emblazoned on the back of their jackets. (Other acronyms were obviously available, so the choice of ICE can be seen as significant.) Immigration attorneys report a toughening of attitudes among ICE trial attorneys as well.

Doris Meissner, who was INS commissioner during the Clinton administration, had issued guidance to the field on prosecutorial discretion. Her memorandum stated that "service officers are not only authorized by law but expected to exercise discretion in a judicious manner at all stages of the enforcement process. . . ." Furthermore, "INS officers may decline to prosecute a legally sufficient immigration case if the Federal immigration enforcement interest that would be served by prosecution is not substantial."[13] Immigration attorneys report that her guidance no longer appears to be in effect in the field, though Hutchinson has stated that the memorandum has not been rescinded and that discretion should continue to be exercised in appropriate situations.[14]

Perhaps even more important than the new toughness is the reorientation of immigration enforcement priorities. Now situated in the DHS, immigration officers are asked to support the central mission of the department: fighting terrorism. Under the old INS, for example, work-site enforcement efforts were targeted at industries that hired large numbers of undocumented migrants. In the DHS, investigators focus on employees at critical infrastructure points, such as nuclear power plants (Operation Glowworm) and airports (Operation Tarmac). INS criminal investigations focused on alien smugglers; ICE is more interested in investigations involving money laundering and violations of export rules linked to materials that can be used in weapons of mass destruction. Indeed, a Department of Justice official noted a degree of competition between ICE and the FBI, with each bureau seeking to be recognized as the preeminent antiterrorism unit in the government. It may well be that in the post–September 11 era it is appropriate for the DHS units to be focused primarily on the war against terrorism. But it is worth noting that the relocation of immigration enforcement activities to the DHS has diminished the pursuit of comprehensive strategies for addressing such immigration-related issues as identifying smuggling routes, removing undocumented migrants, and imposing sanctions on employers who hire undocumented workers. A high-ranking ICE official put it this way: "ICE will perform its immigration mission to carry out the DHS's homeland security mission."[15]

BORDER ENFORCEMENT. After September 11, significant initiatives have been undertaken at the border. Some are plainly focused on terrorism—most obviously the extensive screening and searching of airline passengers carried out by the Transportation Security Administration, the National Security Entry-Exit Registration System, and the new requirement that countries that benefit from the visa-waiver program develop machine-readable passports with biometric indicators.

The DHS announced a major new program in January 2004. Called US-VISIT (United States Visitor and Immigrant Status Indicator Technology), the program requires the electronic collection of biometrics—an inkless "finger-scanning" of both index fingers and a digital photograph—of people arriving at airports on nonimmigrant visas. Congress first mandated development of an entry/exit system in the mid-1990s, when it was widely recognized that the INS had no accurate records for temporary visitors (including whether and when they had left the United States at the end of their authorized stay). Those plans were stalled both for technological reasons and because neighboring countries objected to the huge delays that such a system would impose on land border crossings. In 2000, Congress pressed again for an entry/exit system, and the September 11 attacks accelerated development plans. US-VISIT is the first installment. Undersecretary Hutchinson reports that US-VISIT was unveiled "on time and under budget."

US-VISIT represents a substantial step in gathering information about arriving and departing immigrants. In pilot testing of the program at a few airports, the system identified aliens with criminal records based on their biometrics (a name check would not have found them). It is likely that the new system will deter the entry of some inadmissible noncitizens. And when the program is expanded to capture data on visitors exiting the United States, it will, in theory, be able to produce a database of those overstaying their visas.

A number of concerns, however, should be noted. First, US-VISIT covers only a small proportion (perhaps as few as 6 percent) of the nearly half a billion people who cross U.S. borders each year. Excluded from the program as initially implemented are U.S. citizens, permanent resident aliens (green card holders), temporary visitors who need no visa to enter the United States because they come from one of twenty-seven countries eligible (because of low rates of their nationals overstaying visas) for the visa-waiver program,[16] and residents of Mexico who have border-crossing cards. (The DHS has recently announced that the program will be expanded to cover visitors from visa-waiver countries as of September 30, 2004.)

Currently, the program applies only to noncitizens arriving at airports (roughly 10 percent of the cross-border flow). The DHS has stated that it intends to have US-VISIT operational at the fifty busiest land border ports by December 31, 2004. But the operational difficulties of such an expansion—for example, how to take fingerscans of the millions of noncitizens who enter the United States by car—appear to be significant.

Exit control presents additional challenges. Currently, visitors leaving the United States are required to give air carriers immigration documents that were stapled into their passports on arrival. These are then supposed to be matched up with arrival information, but that has not taken place for years. A full-fledged US-VISIT program would be a significant improvement because an electronic "checkout" system could match biometric entry records. The DHS has announced that it will launch a trial effort to create a departure system via automated, self-service kiosks where visitors with visas will be asked to scan their travel documents and fingerprints. The challenge will be to implement these systems in all ports of departure and to handle the high volume of travelers (particularly at land borders) without creating long delays.

Once fully operational, US-VISIT will help to fill a major gap in immigration enforcement. But its promise is being oversold. While the program will give immigration authorities a far better sense of who is arriving and departing, effective enforcement requires a way to locate and remove those who the system tells us have not departed at the end of their authorized stay. More important, despite administration assertions to the contrary, US-VISIT will not fully safeguard against the entry of terrorists because millions of entering noncitizens will not be covered by the program.[17] Moreover, the DHS has taken no significant steps toward combating the illegal entry of hundreds of thousands of undocumented immigrants each year over the southwestern border.

Hutchinson appears justified in describing the integration of enforcement units from different federal departments as a major accomplishment of the Border and Transportation Safety Directorate's first year. The missions, skills, and cultures of these units were deeply ingrained, and the realignment of agencies in the new department posed a significant challenge.

A great deal of sorting out still needs to be done with respect to priorities, potential conflicts with the FBI, and integration of databases. The Border and Transportation Safety Directorate reports some progress on information sharing among its units, and it recognizes the need for a comprehensive integration of databases. But it is clear that far more work needs to be done on this front, particularly regarding access to databases maintained by the departments of Justice and State, the CIA, and other intelligence organizations. The success of US-VISIT and other entry and exit controls depends on a reliable repository of information that can accurately screen out inadmissible applicants and screen in admissible applicants.

Border and Transportation Safety enforcement priorities will be dominated by national security goals, although day-to-day Border Patrol operations and removal of undocumented immigrants will continue. Indeed, the new, high-tech entry and exit systems will be far more likely to detect immigration violators (those not entitled to enter the United States because of a criminal conviction, fraud, or prior unlawful residence) than potential terrorists, who likely will be knowledgeable about how to avoid setting off the system's alarms.

COORDINATION

As noted, the Homeland Security Act created an asymmetric structure for immigration-related functions at the DHS. The service and enforcement sides report to different people at different levels: the U.S. Citizenship and Immigration Services' director reports to the deputy secretary (the number-two person in the department), while the heads of the enforcement bureaus report to the undersecretary for border and transportation safety (there are five undersecretaries at the DHS). This structure might be sustainable if the units performed wholly unrelated tasks. But they do not. Consider the following examples:

- Under immigration statutes, some noncitizens illegally in the United States may file applications for legal status. Filing an application does not automatically prevent deportation. But, under traditional practice, the INS did not seek to remove someone who had pending a valid claim to remain. The reorganization and USCIS's large and growing backlog of applications now mean that people remain vulnerable to removal far longer, and, because of the separation of the service and enforcement functions, ICE may proceed with removal without consulting with USCIS.

- Individuals seeking asylum here can enter the system in three ways: those arriving at the border may indicate to an inspector (a Customs and Border Protection official) that he or she intends to ask for asylum; noncitizens unlawfully inside the United States and placed in removal proceedings by ICE may file a claim for asylum with an immigration judge; and noncitizens inside the United States not subject to removal proceedings may file an asylum claim with the asylum corps of USCIS. Without coordination, DHS units may be operating under differing understandings of asylum law and policy (and additional interpretations may be injected by immigration judges and the Board of Immigration Appeals, located within the Department of Justice).

◆   Various units in the department make determinations regarding inadmissibility grounds. Border agents evaluate admissibility at time of entry; ICE attorneys may charge someone in the United States with having been "inadmissible at time of entry" (perhaps for entry with fraudulent papers); asylum officers consider some inadmissibility grounds when deciding applications for asylum; USCIS officials do so in making determinations on adjustment of status applications. The applicability and scope of these criteria can raise difficult and important questions of law, as does the granting of waivers of inadmissibility.

The establishment of the separate bureaus also has made locating and contacting the appropriate office to handle a particular policy question far more difficult. Outside groups and even officials at other government departments report frustration in matching issues with bureaus. In some cases, no DHS office will take responsibility. These kinds of problems are the inevitable result of a complex bureaucratic reorganization, and over time responsibilities will be sorted out to a greater extent. But the current complaints suggest that some kind of coordination and public affairs process needs to be organized within the department to help those on the outside navigate its complicated corridors.

Some steps have been taken to achieve internal consistency regarding matters of law. ICE and USCIS have a legal staff, each headed by a legal adviser, and lawyers within these offices consult with one another on issues of mutual interest. The legal advisers report to the DHS general counsel, who frequently convenes meetings with the top lawyers in the department. To be effective, this process needs to be formalized, with clear authority placed in the general counsel's office to resolve differing legal interpretations reached by the various units. The general counsel's office also should ensure consistency in regulation writing—either by serving as a clearinghouse for regulations written by the bureaus or by establishing its own regulation-writing unit.[18]

Formal structures need to be put in place on the policy side as well. The statute creating the department established separate policy units for the service and enforcement bureaus. The Border and Transportation Safety Directorate has an assistant secretary for policy, who can oversee policy development at Customs and Border Protection and Immigration and Customs Enforcement, but coordination between the Border and Transportation Safety Directorate and USCIS appears ad hoc and episodic. It would probably be best to locate a comprehensive immigration policy program in the deputy secretary's office, headed by a counsel to the deputy secretary.

THE ROLE OF THE ATTORNEY GENERAL

The Homeland Security Act placed most immigration functions in the DHS, but it also kept the Executive Office for Immigration Review at the Department of Justice.[19] The Executive Office for Immigration Review includes the Board of Immigration Appeals and several hundred immigration judges who make decisions in entry, removal, and asylum cases. It also houses other administrative law judges who rule on cases brought against employers for hiring undocumented workers or for discriminating against lawful workers. Under Justice Department regulations, the attorney general reserves the power to review Executive Office for Immigration Review decisions. Because the Board of Immigration Appeals considers important questions of immigration law—the scope of removal grounds, asylum law issues, bond determinations—the attorney general's authority ensures that major legal (and policy) decisions will continue to be made at the Department of Justice.

This adds another level of complexity to the already complicated state of immigration law and policymaking. Suppose, for example, that the asylum branch of USCIS has issued a regulation regarding a class of asylum claims. Suppose further that the attorney general has, in a particular case, adopted a different interpretation of the law. The Immigration and Nationality Act declares that rulings by the attorney general "with respect to questions of law shall be controlling."[20] But while that power applies to discrete cases, it is not clear whether the DHS retains authority to issue interpretive regulations that adopt a different view of the law. Furthermore, the Department of Justice and the DHS may disagree on matters of policy that are not strictly legal issues. For instance, because immigration judges make bond determinations, the Justice Department considers it within its authority to make policy on bond-related issues. So, despite the transferring of most immigration functions to the DHS with the intent that the homeland security secretary would be the executive branch's leader on immigration policy, the Homeland Security Act establishes a structure likely to generate discord and uncertainty. Of course, this is not a new phenomenon for executive branch agencies, many of which have duties that overlap and conflict with each other. But it does mean that an interagency process will need to be developed to resolve the disputes that will arise among the departments.[21]

CONCLUSION

Because the September 11 hijackers were noncitizens who had entered the United States through the immigration system, it is not surprising that most immigration functions were transferred to the new DHS. But the result is nonetheless anomalous because the vast majority of immigration regulation and control activities have nothing to do with terrorism. About one million people are granted green cards each year, half a million are naturalized, more than a million are stopped while trying to enter the United States illegally, and tens of thousands of aliens convicted of criminal offenses are deported. No more than a handful of these people are ever linked with terrorist activities.

Has the transfer of immigration functions to the DHS aided in the nation's fight against terrorism? It is hard to say that it has. None of the noncitizens registered under the National Security Entry-Exit Registration System has been prosecuted for links to terrorism; US-VISIT is highly unlikely to identify terrorists seeking entry on tourist visas; and ICE enforcement actions against sexual predators and alien smugglers are not directed at likely terrorists. The administration has asserted that US-VISIT and its proposal to legalize undocumented workers will enhance national security, but these claims are not persuasive.

What these innovations may yield, however, is an immigration system with better information and more integrity. Improved monitoring of population flows across national boundaries, better customer service, and complete criminal and security checks on applicants for immigration benefits are worthy goals; and the division of enforcement and service functions is, on balance, a beneficial reform. But the reorganization will not succeed without a substantial increase in resources to reduce backlogs and to apprehend those who overstay visas, a realistic plan for introducing entry and exit control at borders, accurate information in databases, and technology that integrates databases. Furthermore, no new steps have been taken by the DHS to stop the large and continuous flow of undocumented migrants across America's land borders.

With almost half a billion people crossing U.S. frontiers each year, maintaining a well-regulated border—one that keeps out those not entitled to enter and admits those whose entry is lawful—is a tall order. To the extent that the DHS seeks to craft immigration regulation primarily through the lens of antiterrorism policies, there will be little improvement in the overall functioning of our immigration system. And, while such policies may make Americans feel safer, there also is little reason to believe that they materially advance the war against terrorism.

Appendix

Immigration Functions in the Department of Homeland Security

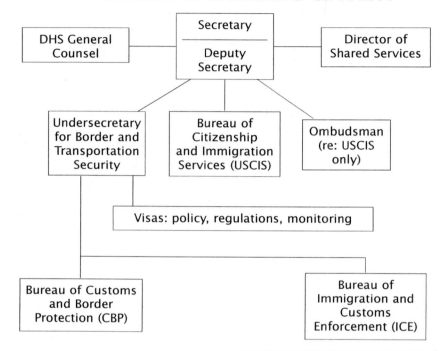

DHS General Counsel: oversees all attorneys in DHS, including approximately six hundred immigration attorneys

USCIS: immigration services, including asylum claims and refugee processing

CBP: border area enforcement, including Border Patrol and inspections

ICE: interior enforcement, including investigations, deportation, detention, and employer sanctions

Not in DHS:

Immigration judges and Board of Immigration Appeals (in Department of Justice)

Care of unaccompanied minors (placed in the Office of Refugee Resettlement, Department of Health and Human Services, by 2003 law)

Consular officers and Bureau of Population, Refugees, and Migration (in Department of State)

Source: David A. Martin, University of Virginia

4.

Strengthening State and Local Terrorism Prevention and Response

Anne M. Khademian

> Our structure of overlapping federal, state and local governance
> . . . provides *unique opportunity* and *challenges* for our home-
> land security efforts. The *opportunity* comes from the expertise
> and commitment of local agencies and organizations involved in
> homeland security. The *challenge* is to develop interconnected and
> complementary systems that are reinforcing rather than duplicative
> and that ensure essential requirements are met. A national strategy
> requires a national effort.
> —*National Strategy for Homeland Security* (emphasis added)
> Office of Homeland Security, July 2002

In its first year, the challenges faced by the Department of Homeland Security (DHS) in working with state and local governments
have been more evident than its accomplishments. On the positive
side, grant money is flowing from the DHS to state governments for
training, planning, and exercises and equipment to prepare first
responders and emergency management professionals; an Initial
National Response Plan was issued in October 2003 to develop the

parameters of coordination and authority in the case of a national emergency across federal, state, and local jurisdictions;[1] efforts to improve the usefulness of the Homeland Security Alert System and the flow of information between the DHS and the states and among local governments are under way;[2] progress has been made to consolidate grant programs within the Office of Domestic Preparedness (ODP) as a "one-stop shop" for states; and the ODP is working to find more effective ways to train first responders.

That progress has been modest, however, because of the ad hoc nature of the approach and its immediate shortcomings. Money continues to be spent without regard to a broad national strategy for preparedness or with much attentiveness to the particular needs of high-risk areas;[3] money is slow to pass from the states to local governments and first responders, many of whom have been bearing huge financial burdens with regard to homeland security; and there is little flexibility in how the money can be spent once first responders receive it.[4] Finally, there remain a host of largely neglected concerns over coordination, communication, and processes for interaction between the DHS, the states, and local governments.

THE DHS APPROACH SO FAR

Several offices within the DHS are focused on working with state and local governments to prevent and respond to terrorist attacks (see Table 4.1). Yet it is difficult to identify an overall strategy to meet this challenge.

Rather than a long-term vision for improving state and local terrorism prevention and response capabilities, DHS administrative practices and the program implementation reflect ad hoc responses to immediate pressures on the young department. The impulse to get grant money rapidly out the door and into the hands of local governments and first responders is intense; it is simply more manageable to establish processes for distributing grants among fifty states than directly to eighty-seven thousand local governments—although this is not necessarily the fastest way to get money to first responders, as experience has demonstrated. As officials in the DHS see it, the prospect of building relationships with individual communities is

TABLE 4.1
DHS OFFICES WITH PRIMARY RESPONSIBILITIES FOR STATE AND LOCAL TERRORISM PREVENTION AND RESPONSE CAPABILITIES

Office	Location in DHS	Purpose
Directorate for Emergency Preparedness and Response (formerly FEMA)	One of five directorates in DHS	To ensure the effectiveness of emergency responders to terrorist attacks, disasters, or other emergencies. To establish a National Incident Management System and a National Response Plan
Office for Domestic Preparedness (ODP)	Directorate for Border and Transportation Security	To prepare the United States for acts of terrorism through grant allocations to states and large urban areas, the provision of training and exercises, access to equipment, coordination, and strategic planning and assistance for the states
Office for State and Local Government Coordination	The Office of the Secretary of DHS	To coordinate DHS state and local programs, assess and advocate for state and local needs, and provide technical support for state and local governments
Office for National Capital Region Coordination	The Office of the Secretary of DHS	To oversee and coordinate federal programs for state, local, and regional authorities in the National Capital Region

overwhelming.[5] The onus is placed instead on the states to take the lead in organizing for homeland security across local jurisdictions. In a department led by former Pennsylvania governor Tom Ridge, and in an administration that advocates state-based federalism,[6] this approach reflects the expectation that states will have more flexibility and autonomy to make policy determinations within their own borders.

To further expedite the grant process, the largest grant programs—formula grants to states based largely on their populations and grants to first responders for training, equipment, and exercises and planning for FY 2004—have been consolidated within the Office for Domestic Preparedness (ODP). For FY 2004, the ODP also has responsibility for the Urban Areas Security Initiative grant programs, training and equipment for firefighters, law enforcement terrorism prevention grants, and grants to encourage community participation.[7] The move transfers responsibility for a significant portion of the training, equipment, and planning and exercise grants from the old Federal Emergency Management Agency (FEMA).[8] The ODP's exclusive emphasis on terrorism prevention and response provides a core focus for the grant program. But that move also slights the long-established capacities of the Directorate for Emergency Preparedness and Response (formerly FEMA), particularly its administration of the grant program for firefighters, and its distribution and monitoring of grants to states and first responders within an "all-hazards" framework that emphasizes preparation for any emergency or disaster.[9]

Finally, the new Office of State and Local Government Coordination (OSLGC) is the primary liaison between the DHS and states, local governments, and organizations that represent state and local officials, first responders, and other emergency management professionals. Legislation pending in the House and Senate would make this office the central contact for all grant programs.[10] But it is understaffed and is still ironing out its mission within the DHS. Currently, a central concern is providing technical support and information primarily through the "Big 7" state and local organizations: the National Association of Counties, National League of Cities, US Conference of Mayors, National Governors Association, Council of State Governments, International City/County Management Association, and the National Conference of State Legislatures.

The fact that the DHS has some semblance of a plan is admirable, considering that it is operating under tremendous expectations to prevent terrorist attacks while ramping up response capabilities fast. But it must do so using grant-making resources that have many congressional strings attached and legacies from three separate departments,[11] administrative systems, and personnel of twenty-two separate entities suddenly flung together, not to mention new offices that remain undefined and understaffed. Opportunities to think strategically, collaboratively, and over the long term have been limited.

In May 2003, for example, the DHS released a draft "National Response Plan" to clarify its roles and responsibilities in coordination with other federal, state, and local agencies in the wake of incidents such as a terrorist attack.[12] When the draft plan was presented at a conference sponsored by the National Emergency Management Association the following month, the reaction of state emergency managers, public health and public works officials, and first responders was negative.[13] State emergency managers, in particular, were concerned that new language, principles, and sources of authority would replace existing response systems and that state and local governments—"the end users"—were not consulted in developing the document.[14] The DHS then took the time to consult with state and local emergency management and first-response professional organizations to produce an "Initial National Response Plan," released on September 30, 2003—outlining a "comprehensive approach to incident management."[15] Reacting to the second draft, one leader of the first-response professional groups who is closely involved in homeland security governance at the regional level argued:

> They [the DHS] truly listened in preparing that document. They put [the first draft] document out and asked for input. . . . and they got a ton of it. . . . I would take it as a bad sign if they only responded by changing a few paragraphs. . . . But they vastly reworked the documents based upon the inputs. . . . It was extraordinary, not rhetoric.[16]

If DHS efforts to rework the National Response Plan are representative, the department has the flexibility for working directly with states and local governments to improve its disaster relief capacities. The question is whether it will be granted sufficient time and resources to do so.

GROWING PAINS

While the DHS has achieved some semblance of a framework for the short term through improvisation, it has already encountered several difficulties:

LACK OF CLEAR, COHERENT PRIORITIES. Critics argue the DHS is spending money without a transparent national strategy for homeland security.[17] At one level, the department has little control over what some view as a pork barrel spending spree.[18] In FY 2004, $1.7 billion of the grants allocated by the DHS will be based on formulas (or "fair shares" for individual states) mandated by Congress. The result is homeland security spending skewed heavily toward states with low populations. In 2003, Wyoming received the most money per capita, $35, while New York and California received approximately $5 per person.[19]

But the problem for the DHS is not so much the fair-share formulas (although the debate over more targeted, risk-based funding is now taking place in Congress), as it is the absence of a scheme for spending the money efficaciously. In 2003, Grand Forks County, North Dakota (population 70,000), received $1.5 million in homeland security funding and was able to purchase the latest equipment to respond to terrorist attacks: biochemical suits, a semiarmored van, decontamination tents, and fully equipped trailers to deal with weapons of mass destruction.[20] The question is whether North Dakota's spending choices were wiser than any alternatives and, if not, how to encourage different decisions there and in other states. Whether in North Dakota, California, or New York, what should a prepared community look like? Does every community need state-of-the-art protective gear and decontaminant capabilities, or is money better spent on training, planning, and coordination? The states are anxiously looking for a "clearly articulated vision" from the DHS for how money should be spent.[21]

OBSTACLES TO REACHING THE FRONT LINES. Local governments, especially in large cities, complain that homeland security funding should go directly to communities and first responders rather than through the states.[22] The money is simply not arriving fast enough, they argue, to alleviate the huge burdens they bear in the homeland security effort.[23] The recently released Gilmore Commission (Advisory Panel to Assess Domestic Response Capabilities for Terrorism Involving Weapons of Mass Destruction) report found that 71 percent of law enforcement organizations and more than half of the paid and volunteer fire departments surveyed confirmed that they had not received any increases in external funding or other resources from Washington or elsewhere.[24] Part of the problem is the administrative lag in devolving grant money back out the statehouse doors to local communities; some states have new offices of homeland security that are understaffed, underfunded, and overworked.[25] Another objection centers on the way public business is routinely conducted: some first-responder organizations view decisions about the allocation of funds made in state capitals as "arbitrary"[26] or based on political considerations rather than calculations of risk or even fair shares. In Michigan, for example, emergency managers from large urban regions complained that their jurisdictions were not represented on the state planning team established to distribute homeland security funds within the state. The numbers tell the story. Oakland County, with 11 percent of the state's population, received only 3 percent of available funds, or approximately $198 for every first responder in the county. In Lansing, the state capital, on the other hand, spending on new equipment for each Michigan state trooper averaged $1,100.[27]

Regardless of these impediments, local governments argue they need more direct financial assistance to shoulder their responsibilities for heightened security alerts and their participation in state homeland security preparedness. The US Conference of Mayors reports that "Code Orange" security alerts cost cities $70 million a week, primarily to pay the overtime for police, firefighters, and other emergency personnel. Costs range from $5 million per week for New York City to $23,000 for Grand Rapids, but the burden is substantial.[28] In addition, local governments are being asked to perform other homeland security–related tasks. In Colorado, the state homeland security office began a survey of critical infrastructure but then assigned local and regional government agencies the duty of completing it.[29]

More direct funding to the local level could help close a preparedness gap among first responders. A report issued by the Council on Foreign Relations found first responders poorly equipped and poorly trained to meet the demands of an emergency brought on by a terrorist attack. Less than 10 percent of fire departments in the United States have the training and equipment needed to deal with a building collapse. Police departments in major cities lack the equipment to secure a site after an attack with weapons of mass destruction. And most cities are in want of the instruments needed to determine the type of hazardous materials first responders might face.[30] A recent report by FEMA found similar evidence of equipment scarcity and insufficient training. Nearly 40 percent of firefighters who would be responsible for responding to a situation involving hazardous materials have not received appropriate training and 75 percent of firefighters cannot find the means to communicate with other first responders at the federal, state, and local levels.[31]

A CUMBERSOME GRANT-AWARDING PROCESS. The other major criticism related to DHS funding is the complexity of the grant process and the lack of flexibility in spending the money. Representative Christopher Cox (R-CA), chairman of the House Select Committee on Homeland Security, refers to the application process for first-responder funding as a "convoluted 12-step process to receive a portion of the money Congress has already made available."[32] According to Representative Cox and other critics, the grant application process should be more direct and the available funding streams less fragmented. By consolidating first-responder grant programs within the ODP, the DHS has taken a step toward creating a one-stop shop, but the programs remain separate, requiring multiple layers of applications.[33]

An additional problem is the lack of flexibility in first responders' use of the funds. In testimony before the Senate Governmental Affairs Committee, the chief of police of Dover, Delaware, presented the challenges facing first responders waiting for their share of grants channeled through the state:

> You need to know that those resources do not go directly to local police departments. They cannot be used to hire new police. They cannot be used to pay overtime expenses that we incur each and every time Secretary Ridge changes the alert level. They can be used to purchase equipment, but not by me. I have to wait for a state-wide plan to be developed and then I have to hope that a fair share of those funds will filter to my department.[34]

INADEQUATE COORDINATION AND COMMUNICATION. Finally, the DHS has so far failed to resolve issues relating to coordination across federal, state, and local governments, as well as improved communications systems that would promote cooperation on a national scale.[35] In May 2003, the DHS (through the Office of Domestic Preparedness) conducted TOPOFF2, a five-day exercise featuring top government officials that simulated a bioterrorism attack in Chicago and a dirty-bomb explosion in Seattle. Evaluations of the exercise revealed significant coordination and communication problems. Most prominent were problems with the Homeland Security Alert System, which did not work properly with existing state protocols.[36] According to an internal report, "disagreement resulted between local, state, and federal agencies over whether the DHS has implemented 'Orange' or 'Red,' and whether the level was applicable nationally or locally."[37] Another assessment of the exercise noted, "Unquestionably, a substantial gap exists between the homeland security concept of a red alert and local officials'." In reference to a federal decision to "shut down" the country for one or two days during the TOPOFF2 exercise, this insider's assessment continued:

> At the time, we were trying to reassure the Central Puget Sound population that many areas were in fact safe, the federal government seemed to be saying that not only were Seattle and Chicago not safe, but also that the bowling alley in Moberly, Missouri, and the delicatessen in Winona, Minnesota, were in danger.[38]

A range of other problems also surfaced. In Seattle there was confusion over the forward coordinating team for FEMA and the role of new personnel sent to represent the DHS on the ground; there were no standard, accepted procedures for federal, state, and local authorities to jointly release public information; and the absence of established protocols, training, and guidelines negatively affected efforts to request disaster medical supplies and remote sensing equipment from the federal government, as well as the communication of technical information about radiation to nontechnical personnel at the federal, state, and local levels.[39] The TOPOFF2 exercise, in short, revealed a long list of items that will require the DHS to link and standardize communication among federal, state, and local governments; facilitate transfers of medical and other equipment from federal agencies to local governments; and provide training across jurisdictions for different categories of emergency professionals.[40]

The problems of coordination, communication, and procedural stumbling blocks can by no means all be attributed to the intricacies of federalism. Recent reports by The Century Foundation focused on homeland security challenges within individual states found similar challenges within and between local jurisdictions.[41] Pennsylvania, for example, has no statewide incident management system to integrate an emergency response.[42] Three counties in Wisconsin near a nuclear power plant have no stockpiles of potassium iodide for use in a nuclear emergency because of disagreements over the costs and liabilities of storage.[43] Incompatible communication equipment across local jurisdictions and among different agencies within the same jurisdiction remains a critical coordination problem within the state of Washington.[44] And in Indiana, according to a report in *Stateline.org*, an online magazine, a state law mandates mutual aid agreements for all ninety-two counties and establishes a catalog of all emergency equipment, but "the state has no way of making first responders in each county purchase equipment that will work in harmony with other counties."[45] While these issues might be perceived by the DHS as minutiae to be remedied by states and regional entities, greater attention to emergency standards of preparedness in the DHS plan for working with state and local governments would provide essential guidance for coordination at the local and regional levels.

UNDERLYING CHALLENGES FOR IMPROVEMENT

The challenge to the DHS proffered in the *National Strategy for Homeland Security* is to "develop interconnected and complimentary systems that are reinforcing rather than duplicative and that ensure essential requirements are met. A national strategy requires a national effort."[46] To meet it will require resolving three fundamental issues:

WHETHER AN "ALL-HAZARDS" APPROACH SHOULD GUIDE POLICY. Central to a successful partnership with state and local governments will be defining the relationship between established systems of emergency management and the new responsibilities of homeland security. Over the past decade, emergency management at the federal level has moved toward an all-hazards approach. Rather than focusing on planning and preparation for different types of emergencies—from hurricanes and tornadoes to toxic chemical spills, fires, or terrorist attacks—emergency professionals focus on the functions of emergency management: *mitigation* (reducing the impact of future disasters), *preparedness* (training, technical assistance, and exercises), and *response and recovery* (immediate action following a disaster followed by restoration of the community). States and communities as well have gradually moved toward this all-hazards approach over the past decade with the support, cajoling, and grant guidance from, first, FEMA and, then, its institutional successor, the DHS Directorate of Emergency Preparedness and Response. State emergency managers have added their support in making the transition. FEMA's efforts to establish uniform standards of all-hazards emergency management capabilities provided state governments with a means to benchmark their progress and to identify the gaps in emergency preparedness.[47]

Homeland security adds two priorities to this all-hazards mix: an emphasis on terrorist attacks as a type of manmade disaster and a focus on prevention, awareness, and mitigation. The question for many state and local officials is how the two concepts fit together. Is emergency management an element of homeland security, or is homeland security an element of emergency management? For many first responders, homeland security is a natural extension of the broader all-hazards approach. Fire and rescue teams, for example, need to know how to deal with a building collapse or a chemical explosion regardless of whether the incident was caused by a terrorist attack or an accident.

But there are some important differences between an all-hazards approach to preparedness and one built around a specific emphasis on terrorism. Consider law enforcement. If preparedness is framed in terms of preventing and responding to terrorist attacks, law enforcement officials must be focused on counterterrorism activities like identifying threats and building interagency relationships for information sharing and investigation. After an attack, law enforcement capabilities must be focused on securing and investigating the crime scene. When the organizational strategy emphasizes an all-hazards framework, prevention and investigation are less prominent than efforts to secure roads, evacuate, and prevent looting. Further, the equipment that first responders need to respond to a terrorist attack involving weapons of mass destruction—particle detectors, protective gear, breathing apparatuses, and so forth—require additional training beyond that provided under an all-hazards system.

Perhaps most critical are the differences in the prominence of one type of uniformed personnel or another and the distribution of dollars when a specific approach is emphasized. Largely because of prevention responsibilities, concentrating on terrorism favors state and local police departments in homeland security planning. The fire chief from Alachua County, Florida, is not alone when he counts "many more police badges than fire fighters uniforms" at homeland security task force meetings.[48] The tilt toward law enforcement also was noted when the DHS began organizing for a national response plan. As Alan Caldwell of the International Fire Chiefs Association commented, "We're the last to be consulted. Yet, in an incident, we'll be the first to respond."[49] In contrast, under the all-hazards framework, firefighters have had their own direct grant program for equipment and training, Assistance to Firefighters. Despite their opposition, this program has been consolidated within the Office of Domestic Prevention for 2004 so that the money is channeled through state offices along with all other homeland security funding.[50]

Historically the federal government has struggled over the relationship between programs aimed at responding primarily to natural disasters and those focused on national security (or civil emergency) preparedness.[51] The transformation of FEMA in the 1990s to effective leadership is largely attributed to the separation of the agency's all-hazards capability from its longtime civil emergency capacity.[52] Former FEMA director James Lee Witt's opposition to the subsuming of the agency by the DHS was based on the concern that FEMA's all-hazards capacity would be diminished by the greater emphasis on preventing and responding to a terrorist attack.[53] The reaction of state emergency managers to the first draft of the National Response Plan as "slanted toward terrorism-specific incidents" revealed a similar concern about the need to maintain a strong all-hazards approach: "We know that the possibility for natural disasters and emergencies to occur far exceeds the possibility for terrorist events."[54]

The DHS weighed in with its Initial National Response Plan, calling for a "single all-discipline, all-hazards plan."[55] But how terrorism prevention and response fits within the all-hazards, all-discipline framework is not clear. The two primary sources of state and local funding within the DHS reinforce a division between all-hazards and terrorism. Over the past decade, FEMA sponsored the all-hazards emergency approach through grants, training programs, and technical support for the states and local governments. Now called the Directorate of Emergency Preparedness and Response, the division is charged with "protect[ing] the Nation from all-hazards by leading and supporting the Nation in a comprehensive risk-based emergency management program."[56] In the fiscal year 2003 budget, FEMA was tapped to manage $3.5 billion for first-responder training, equipment, exercises, and statewide planning.[57] Homeland security functions focused on terrorism, in other words, were to be directed through an all-hazards framework.

Yet, in the FY 2004 budget, funding for homeland security preparedness functions—first responder training, equipment, planning, and exercises—has gone primarily to the ODP.[58] The ODP is charged with the "primary responsibility within the executive branch of government for the preparedness of the United States for acts of terrorism."[59]

The perception that different offices support divergent approaches for distinct types of preparedness is problematic. The federal emergency management Web site, for example, still identifies the agency as "FEMA," rather than the Directorate for Emergency Preparedness and Response. One is hard-pressed to find a link to the DHS or to the ODP on the Web page.[60] Similarly, several Web links for the ODP, including links for technical support and grant information, are still located at the ODP's previous Department of Justice Web address.[61] These subtle reminders of contrasting priorities between an all-hazards approach and preparedness for terrorism bedevil state and local governments as well. In selecting a strategy for homeland security implementation, governors and state emergency management personnel are naturally drawn to the money available through the ODP to prepare for a terrorist attack.[62] To the extent that a separate director of homeland security at the state level serves as the focal point for coordinating a state's planning and application for ODP funding rather than an established office of emergency management, the barrier between an all-hazards approach and a developing emphasis on terrorism prevention is transferred to the state level.

At this point, it is not clear what the best approach is. Should terrorism prevention and response capabilities be integrated within an all-hazards framework—a baseline system of readiness for any type of disaster, with the capacity to respond to the extraordinary? Or should the focus be on homeland security, which would entail ramping up law enforcement for counterterrorism capabilities and investigation, delivering specialized equipment and training to first responders relating to the use of weapons of mass destruction, and treating existing emergency management systems as the response component of a broader security framework?

A fundamental challenge for the DHS is to find a way to conceptualize and communicate the relationship between emergency all-hazards management and homeland security priorities to state and local governments. Indeed, clarity is essential for defining community baseline capacities for preparedness (national standards), particularly in order to provide flexibility for regional needs.[63]

WHAT DOES THE DHS EXPECT AND NEED FROM STATE AND LOCAL GOVERNMENTS? States, local governments, and first responders want three basic things from the DHS. First, they need better information to accompany changes in the Homeland Security Alert System. As one DHS official put it, "They want information for what it is we know that they may need to know."[64] Second, they want to be included in efforts to develop homeland security policy that affects the work of emergency managers and first responders. Third, they are calling for money for improving preparedness and covering the cost of mobilizing personnel and systems in response to the more elevated color codes.

What the DHS wants from state and local governments and first responders, however, remains fuzzy. Are states and local government to be active collaborators in the homeland security effort? If the swift and negative reaction to the first draft of the National Response Plan is any indication, the DHS cannot dictate policy and expect implementation by the states. Rather, if the department expects states and local governments to be strategic partners, it needs to accommodate them in concrete ways.

The DHS now places a tremendous burden on state governments to conduct their own strategic planning. The Office of Domestic Preparedness requires, for fiscal year 2004 funding, each state to prepare a State Homeland Security Strategy based on assessments of local and state needs and risks and focused on goals and objectives to enhance terrorism prevention, response, and recovery. The ODP will then work with states to craft a State Assistance Plan to guide the ODP training, equipment, exercise, technical support, and other forms of help.[65]

Yet states are experiencing great difficulties in carrying the weight of those responsibilities. While many states have established programs or offices of homeland security as their point of contact with the DHS, some have not allocated money to homeland security functions and are instead relying on the grant money from the DHS for support.[66] Some states, such as Virginia, have managed to fund a robust strategic planning venture with grant money from a variety of federal sources, yet the mandate to pass on 80 percent of homeland security grant money to localities leaves little for most state offices to work with.[67]

The ODP does provide some help for developing strategic plans. There is a template on its Web page,[68] and it provides ongoing technical support for states. ODP officials also travel and speak at conferences focused on state and local emergency management to relay information about assistance that is in the pipeline and other issues. Expectations for how these interactions take place can be incompatible. From the perspective of the ODP, the responsibility of states to develop a plan forces them to engage in the kind of reevaluation necessary to increase the capacity of first responders and to think strategically about prevention. This cannot help but encourage exchanges across jurisdictions and state agencies, among first responders, and with the DHS through the technical support process. Areas requiring greater coordination and mutual aid agreements between jurisdictions also should be identified. If each state is able to develop a plan, that should enable the ODP to focus on a single office or director for coordinating homeland security resources.[69]

But it takes time for states to assess their vulnerabilities and needs. Building relationships with other jurisdictions to create organizational cooperation and coordination also takes time—lots of time.[70] Many local communities do not have the means to free up their fire and police chiefs, for example, from their day-to-day management responsibilities. Many state emergency managers face similar challenges. If the DHS expects states and local governments to be strategic partners, resources geared explicitly to relationship building and strategic planning need to be available.

A model for building strategic partnerships with state and local governments is the one in place for the national capital region—the District of Columbia and surrounding counties in Virginia and Maryland. An extensive study of the emergency response by Arlington County, Virginia, to the terrorist attack on the Pentagon on September 11, 2001, focused in part on routine but critical working relationships between officials at the local, state, and federal levels.[71] Several lubricants facilitate the complex mechanics of these relationships, including administrative support for first-responder functions within individual counties—human resources staff, budget and planning, and purchasing—that allows police and fire chiefs, for example, some opportunity to participate at a regional level in coordination and planning efforts.[72]

The keen interest of the federal government in a secure national capital region clearly drove the process of coordination. A special provision in the Homeland Security Act created a separate Office for National Capital Region Coordination within the secretary's office in the DHS that is charged with overseeing and coordinating "federal programs for and relationships with State, local and regional authorities in the National Capital Region."[73] No other region has a similar office. Also noteworthy is the FBI's National Capital Response Squad, which consists of leaders from FBI specialist teams who routinely confer with local fire chiefs, hazardous material personnel, police chiefs, and others to coordinate the work of the bureau with first responders in the event of an attack or disaster requiring federal investigation.

Finally, the national capital region benefits from the support of the Metropolitan Washington Council of Governments (COG). Broadly, the COG supports the National Capital Region Emergency Preparedness Council, composed of elected officials across the region, leaders of police, fire, health, and other emergency response personnel, directors of emergency management, and others to oversee and implement the Regional Emergency Coordination Plan. The COG also supports the work of professional and technical committees, involving the fire chiefs, police chiefs, and public health officials, providing forums for planning across first-responder communities.[74]

The national capital region is unique, but if the DHS expects state and local governments to be genuine partners in the homeland security effort, it provides a model. Through the support work of the Office of State and Local Coordination, the Directorate of Emergency Preparedness and Response, and the ODP, the DHS can encourage the use of metropolitan councils of governments, provide resources for support staff and planning efforts, and perhaps consider organizing the DHS resources or offices around specific regions similar to the national capital region.

WHAT DOES CONGRESS WANT? Ultimately any DHS plan for working with state and local governments must mesh with congressional expectations for the department. Both houses of Congress care deeply about how homeland security money is spent, and demands that the money be allocated on a fair-share basis—what many view as a little "pork" for everyone—compete with efforts to target scarce resources on high-risk areas. Two bills recently introduced by different committees capture the debate. Each bill presents contrasting approaches to grant distribution, with different advocates, and presents its own set of challenges to the DHS for the distribution and spending of homeland security grant money (Table 4.2, page 114). For Congress, the eventual prominence of one idea over the other also will cause a realignment in the constellation of congressional committees with jurisdiction over homeland security.

The House Select Committee on Homeland Security and its pending legislation, "Faster and Smarter Funding for First Responders of 2003," represents the risk-based approach. The legislation has three priorities.

◆ The grant application process would be faster because it would be streamlined or simplified from its current twelve-step process.

◆ Spending would be "smarter" because it would be targeted to regions, states, or multistate areas deemed to be at higher risk of a terrorist attack. The DHS Directorate of Information Analysis and Infrastructure Protection would participate in determining the risk levels of different applicants.

◆ With the incentive of faster funding for first responders, governments across a region could work together and apply directly to the DHS for emergency preparedness support.[75]

Large cities that are more vulnerable to a terrorist attack—and first responders interested in direct applications to the DHS for funding—are the primary advocates of the bill.

In contrast, the Senate Governmental Affairs Committee produced an alternative approach to funding through the recently introduced Homeland Security Grant Enhancement Act of 2003.

◆   The bill firmly establishes states as the pivot for grant applications and distributions.

◆   Each state would receive a fair share of grant money based upon population formulas. Grants would be consolidated via a central clearinghouse, with the Office of State and Local Government Coordination as the single point of contact for grant applications.[76]

Governors, state emergency management officials, and newly established offices of homeland security at the state level are the primary advocates for this approach.

These two starkly different approaches have fundamental implications for the development of the DHS. A targeted approach to funding would alter the relationship between the DHS and the states. First responders, mayors, and regional planning consortiums would compete directly with governors and state homeland security advisers for DHS attention and resources. It also would elevate demands on the DHS's analytic and intelligence-gathering capabilities by requiring the Directorate of Information Analysis and

TABLE 4.2
TWO CONGRESSIONAL APPROACHES TO DHS GRANT DISTRIBUTION

	Risk Based	Fair Share
Committee in Congress and representative legislation	◆ House Select Committee on Homeland Security ◆ "Faster and Smarter Funding for First Responders," HR 3266	◆ Senate Governmental Affairs Committee ◆ Homeland Security Grant Enhancement Act, S. 1245
Grant targets	◆ Major metropolitan areas or other regions that work together to plan and prepare ◆ States ◆ Multistate applicants	◆ States

TABLE 4.2

	Risk Based	Fair Share
Core ideas	◆ Grant money should be linked to vulnerabilities, should be directed to communities, states, and regions that demonstrate ability to plan and prepare across jurisdictions, and should reach first responders rapidly	◆ In a federal system, states should have the ability to plan, coordinate, and build homeland security approaches that reflect particular vulnerabilities within broader national parameters, and should be able to access funding through a streamlined process
Primary advocates	◆ First responders ◆ Large cities	◆ Governors ◆ State homeland security advisers
Administrative challenge for DHS	◆ Developing expertise in risk analysis that can be linked to grant determinations ◆ Coordinating and working with the states and with diverse units of government	◆ Working with governors and state homeland security directors/advisers to address the needs of a state and its first responders
Administrative challenge for state and local governments	◆ Determining how best to organize for homeland security funding—multistate, state, or regional coordination ◆ Developing the capacity to conduct ongoing determinations of vulnerabilities, needs, risk	◆ Developing a statewide homeland security strategy that can guide spending at the local level ◆ Distributing the money to local governments and first responders in a timely and strategic manner

Infrastructure Protection to conduct independent assessments of risk for regional applicants. Finally, under the targeted resource approach, the DHS would be required to play a more active role in determining what it means for a community or region to be prepared—a baseline of preparedness.

The fair-share approach would promote a more traditional view of federalism, deferring to each state and reinforcing the relationships the DHS is building with individual statehouses. As an administrator of grant money, the DHS would play a role in coordinating and supporting independent state efforts rather than directly carrying out analysis and strategic allocation.

The two alternatives also have significant effects on how state and local governments organize for federal assistance. Under a targeted approach to grants, states and local jurisdictions would need to collaborate on planning and preparedness and on finding the best way to secure adequate homeland security funding. While states would still be able to apply directly for money, there would be the option to apply to the DHS through a regional consortium or a multistate alliance. Individual states, intrastate regions, or coalitions of states would need to develop and sustain the capacity to conduct ongoing determinations of vulnerabilities and needs.

Under the fair-share approach, states would confront the same challenges they face today. They would need to develop a State Homeland Security Strategy to guide spending and preparedness across jurisdictions and figure out ways to distribute money to local governments and first responders in a timely and strategic manner.

Currently, thirteen committees in the House and eleven committees in the Senate have jurisdiction over homeland security issues. The creation of the House Select Committee on Homeland Security represents an attempt at strategic consolidation of legislative initiatives relating to homeland security issues, with membership drawn from other committees with homeland security oversight responsibilities. Should a version of "Faster and Smarter Funding" be put into law, the clout of the select committee would be magnified. Congressional overlap has long been the bane of reformers interested in a more "clean" and precise policy process. It is not going away any time soon, but a more coherent approach to homeland security policymaking and funding could result from a bill that emphasizes targeted funding over pork barrel spending.

THE BOTTOM LINE

The big question is whether the nation is better prepared with the DHS in the picture. Shortcomings of the current DHS plan for improving the terrorism prevention and response capabilities of state and local governments include spending without an overarching strategy, complex processes for securing grants, a trickle-down pace for the distribution of money, a lack of flexibility in spending that money, and a multitude of problems related to communication and coordination. The DHS, and Congress, must tackle three challenges in order to better its working relationships with state and local government: defining which takes precedence between all-hazards emergency management and an approach that subsumes all preparations under homeland security; clarifying the expectations the DHS has for state and local governments; and reaching a political consensus about what should be accomplished with homeland security policy and spending. The DHS can help by deepening its involvement with state and local governments and by hammering out its priorities with members of Congress. How the DHS grapples with these issues will go a long way in determining the sophistication and quality of its campaign to enlist state and local governments in the building of a system of national preparedness.

NOTES

OVERVIEW

1. "Radio Address by the President to the Nation," White House, June 8, 2002, transcript available online at http://www.whitehouse.gov/news/releases /2002/06/20020608-1.html.

2. *A Review of Background Checks for Federal Passenger and Baggage Screeners at Airports,* OIG-04-08, Office of Inspections, Evaluations, and Special Reviews, Office of Inspector General, Department of Homeland Security, January 2004, available online at http://www.dhs.gov/interweb /assetlibrary/OIG-04-08_ReviewofScreenerBackgroundChecks.pdf.

3. "Aviation Security: Vulnerabilities and Potential Improvements for the Air Cargo System," GAO-03-344, U.S. General Accounting Office, December 2002, available online at http://www.gao.gov/new.items/d03344.pdf.

4. Hudson Morgan, "Shipping News," *New Republic,* July 7–14, 2003, p. 10.

5. Statement of Cathleen A. Berrick, director, Homeland Security and Justice, before the Committee on Government Reform, U.S. Congress, House, "Aviation Security: Efforts to Measure Effectiveness and Strengthen Security Programs," GAO-04-285T, U.S. General Accounting Office, November 20, 2003, available online at http://www.gao.gov/new.items/d04285t.pdf.

6. Statement of Robert F. Dacey, director, Information Security Issues, before the Subcommittee on Cybersecurity, Science, and Research and Development and the Subcommittee on Infrastructure and Border Security, U.S. Congress, House, Select Committee on Homeland Secuity, "Homeland Security: Information Sharing Responsibilities, Challenges, and Key Management Issues," GAO-03-1165T, U.S. General Accounting Office, September 17, 2003, available online at http://www.gao.gov/new.items /d031165t.pdf.

7. *Creating a Trusted Network for Homeland Security: Second Report of the Markle Foundation Task Force,* Task Force on National Security in the Information Age, Markle Foundation, New York, December 2003, p. 3, available online at http://www.markletaskforce.org/Report2_Full_Report.pdf.

8. Mimi Hall, "Homeland Security Money Doesn't Match Terror Threat: Does Zanesville, Ohio, Need to Test for Nerve Agents as NY Struggles for Funds?" *USA Today,* October 29, 2003, p. 1A, available online at http://www .usatoday.com/news/washington/2003-10-29-security-cover-usat_x.htm.

9. *Forging America's New Normalcy: Securing Our Homeland, Protecting Our Liberty,* Fifth Annual Report to the President and Congress of the Advisory Panel to Assess Domestic Response Capabilities for Terrorism Involving Weapons of Mass Destruction (Gilmore Commission), December 15, 2003, Appendix D, p. D-2-3, available online at http://www.rand.org /nsrd/terrpanel/volume_v/volume_v_appendices_only.pdf.

10. See Department of Homeland Security, "Top Officials (TOPOFF) Exercise Series: TOPOFF 2—After Action Summary Report for Public Release," December 19, 2003, available online at http://www.dhs.gov/interweb /assetlibrary/T2_Report_Final_Public.doc.

11. Statement of Norman J. Ornstein, resident scholar, American Enterprise Institute, before the Subcommittee on Rules, U.S. Congress, House, Select Committee on Homeland Security, "Perspectives on House Reform of Homeland Security: Lessons from the Past," 108th Cong., 1st sess., May 19, 2003, available online at http://www.aei.org/news/newsID.17514/news _detail.asp.

CHAPTER 1

1. Greg Schneider and Sara Kehaulani Goo, "Twin Missions Overwhelmed TSA," *Washington Post,* September 3, 2002, p. A1.

2. Steven Brill, *After: How America Confronted the September 12 Era* (New York: Simon and Schuster, 2003), p. 105.

3. "U.S. Representative Harold Rogers (R-KY) Holds Hearing on Transportation Security," U.S. Congress, House, Committee on Appropriations, Subcommittee on Transportation, FDCH Political Transcripts, Federal Document Clearing House, Inc., Washington, D.C., June 20, 2002.

4. Greg Schneider and Sara Kehaulani Goo, "Screening Deadline Worries Grow," *Washington Post,* June 14, 2002, p. A9.

5. Ibid.

6. "Federal Security Screeners Successfully Deployed at All U.S. Airports," press release, Transportation Security Administration, November 18, 2002, available online at http://www.tsa.gov/public/display?theme=44&content =0900051980031db7.

7. Statement of Gerald L. Dillingham, director, physical infrastructure issues, before the Committee on Commerce, Science and Transportation, U.S. Congress, Senate, "Aviation Security: Transportation Security Administration Faces Immediate and Long-Term Challenges," GAO-02-971T, U.S. General Accounting Office, July 25, 2002, available online at http://www.gao.gov/new.items/d02971t.pdf.

8. Sara Kehaulani Goo, "TSA under Pressure to Stop Baggage Theft," *Washington Post*, June 29, 2003, p. A1.

9. Sara Kehaulani Goo, "Airport Finds that More Screeners Are Questionable, *Washington Post,* June 12, 2003, p. A3.

10. "U.S. Representative Christopher Cox (R-CA) Holds Hearing on Homeland Security Progress," U.S. Congress, House, Select Homeland Security Committee, FDCH Political Transcripts, Federal Document Clearing House, Inc., Washington, D.C., May 20, 2003, p. 12; Philip Shenon, "Report Faults Lax Controls on Screeners at Airports," *New York Times*, February 6, 2004.

11. "Hiring Practices for the Transportation Security Administration's (TSA) Screener Workforce," hearing of the Homeland Security Subcommittee, U.S. Congress, House, Appropriations Committee, 108th Cong., 1st sess., Federal News Service, June 3, 2003.

12. "Airport Passenger Screening: Preliminary Observations on Progress Made and Challenges Remaining," Report to the Chairman, Subcommittee on Aviation, U.S. Congress, House, Committee on Transportation and Infrastructure, GAO-03-1173, U.S. General Accounting Office, September 24, 2003, available online at http://www.gao.gov/new.items/d031173.pdf.

13. Matthew L.Wald, "Official Says Airport Trainees Knew Questions before Tests," *New York Times*, October 8, 2003.

14. Ibid.

15. "Air Travelers' Security Enhanced as TSA Intercepts Over 4.8 Million Prohibited Items in First Year, Including 1,101 Firearms," press release, Transportation Security Administration, U.S. Department of Homeland Security, March 10, 2003, available online at http://www.tsa.gov /public/display?theme=44&content=0900051980018d06.

16. "Artfully Concealed Items Confiscated by TSA Screeners," press release, Transportation Security Administration, U.S. Department of Homeland Security, August 25, 2003, available online at http://www.tsa .gov/public/display?theme=44&content=0900051980085e4d.

17. "Air Travelers' Security Enhanced."

18. "Airport Passenger Screening: Preliminary Observations."

19. Maki Becker and Greg Gittrich, "Weapons Still Fly at Airports," New York *Daily News*, September 4, 2002, p. 7.

20. Roger McCoy, "Airport Security Test Finds Faulty Screenings," *Columbus Dispatch*, July 29, 2003, p. 4B.

21. Sara Kehaulani Goo, "TSA to Check Plane Inspections," *Washington Post*, October 22, 2003, p. A10.

22. "Holes in TSA's Screens," *Washington Post*, October 22, 2003, p. A28.

23. "Airport Passenger Screening: Preliminary Observations."

24. "Hearing on Aviation Security," U.S. Congress, Senate, Commerce Committee, Aviation Subcommittee, FDCH Political Transcripts, Federal Document Clearing House, Inc., Washington, D.C., February 5, 2003.

25. "Oversight of Security Contracts," letter from James M. Loy, undersecretary of transportation for security, to Kenneth M. Mead, inspector general, U.S. Department of Transportation, January 21, 2003, available online at http://www.oig.dot.gov/item_details.php?item=1028.

26. Letter from Alexis M. Stefani, principal assistant inspector general for auditing and evaluation, U.S. Department of Transportation, to James M. Loy, undersecretary of transportation for security, February 28, 2003, available online at http://www.oig.dot.gov/item_details.php?item=1028.

27. "U.S. Representative Christopher Cox Holds Hearing," p. 12.

28. Cheryl Fiandaca, "Airport Screeners Live It Up at Taxpayer Expense," WABC-TV News, New York, May 7, 2003, available online at http://abclocal.go.com/wabc/news/wabc_050703_airscreeners.html; Tom Ramstack, "Investigators Audit Expenses of Arlington, VA, Airport Security Contractor," *Washington Times*, July 17, 2003; Leslie Miller, "Perks of Air Screeners' Trainers Probed," *Washington Post*, July 16, 2003.

29. Stephen Barr, "A Vow to Closely Oversee Personnel Management Contracts," *Washington Post*, July 31, 2003, p. B2.

30. Sara Kehaulani Goo, "Large, Small Airports to Use Different Security Systems," *Washington Post*, March 28, 2002, p. A5.

31. Statement of Cathleen A. Berrick, director, Homeland Security and Justice, before the Committee on Government Reform, U.S. Congress, House, "Aviation Security: Efforts to Measure Effectiveness and Strengthen Security Programs," GAO-04-285T, U.S. General Accounting Office, November 20, 2003, available online at http://www.gao.gov/new.items/d04285t.pdf.

32. Ibid.

33. Robert O'Harrow, Jr., "TSA Modifies Screening Plan," *Washington Post*, June 14, 2003, p. E1.

34. James M. Loy, "Privacy Will Be Protected," *USA Today*, March 12, 2003, p. 12A; O'Harrow, "TSA Modifies Screening Plan."

35. Stephen Power, "TSA Chief Pushes Screening System," *Wall Street Journal* abstracts, September 29, 2003, p. A12.

36. Philip Shenon, "Airline Gave Defense Firm Passenger Files," *New York Times*, September 20, 2003, p. A1.

37. Sara Kehaulani Goo, "TSA May Try to Force Airlines to Share Data," *Washington Post*, September 27, 2003, p. A11.

38. Sara Kehaulani Goo, "Northwest Gave U.S. Data on Passengers: Airline Had Denied Sharing Information for Security Effort," *Washington Post*, January 18, 2004, p. A1.

39. Transportation Security administrator James Loy was appointed deputy secretary at the Department of Homeland Security on October 23, 2003. Rear Admiral David M. Stone replaced Loy on December 4, 2004, as TSA's acting administrator.

40. Statement of Cathleen A. Berrick, "Aviation Security: Efforts to Measure Effectiveness."

41. Mary Schiavo, with Sabra Chartrand, *Flying Blind, Flying Safe: The Former Inspector General of the U.S. Department of Transportation Tells You Everything You Need to Know to Travel Safer by Air* (New York: Avon Books, 1997).

42. The exact number of air marshals is classified information. However, *USA Today* reporter Blake Morrison wrote, "Although the precise number of marshals is classified, sources say about 6,000 have been hired since Sept. 11." Blake Morrison, "Air Marshal Program in Disarray, Insiders Say," *USA Today*, August 15, 2002, p. 1A. Another story, run four months later, put the air marshal force at "more than 4,000." See "Air Marshals Reveal Security Lapses," *USA Today*, December 24, 2002, p. 11A.

43. Greg Schneider and Sara Kehaulani Goo, "For Air Marshals, a Steep Takeoff," *Washington Post*, January 2, 2003, p. A1; Blake Morrison, "Air Marshals' Resignations Flood TSA, Managers Say," *USA Today*, August 29, 2002, p. 1A; Morrison, "Air Marshal Program in Disarray."

44. Sara Kehaulani Goo, "Customs Agents to Be Marshals," *Washington Post*, September 3, 2003, p. A6.

45. "General Aviation: Status of Industry, Related Infrastructure, and Safety Issues," GAO-01-916, U.S. General Accounting Office, August 2001, available online at http://www.aviationtoday.com/reports/status0801.pdf.

46. Joseph A. Kinney, "Clamp Down on General Aviation," *Washington Post*, September 25, 2001, p. A23.

47. Kathleen Koch, "Police: Tampa Pilot Voiced Support for bin Laden, CNN.com/U.S., January 7, 2002, available online at http://www.cnn.com /2002/US/01/06/tampa.crash/.

48. Greg Griffin, "Flight Risks? Little Has Been Done to Boost Security at the Nation's General Aviation Airports," *Denver Post*, August 17, 2003, p. K1.

49. Ibid.

50. See the Web site of the Aircraft Owners and Pilots Association, Frederick, Md., available online at http://www.aopa.org.

51. See the Web site of the Center for Responsive Politics, Washington, D.C., available online at http://www.opensecrets.org. Thirteen organizations gave $10,000 or more to Oberstar's 2002 campaign: National Air Traffic Controllers, Airline Pilots Association, Aircraft Owners and Pilots Association, Amalgamated Transit Union, FedEx, Machinist/Aerospace Workers Union, Professional Airways Systems Specialists, Teamsters, Transportation Communication Union, UPS, United Transportation Union, Laborers Union, and American Federation of State, County, and Municipal Employees.

52. James Oberstar, "Resolution: To Commend the Aircraft Owners and Pilots Association on Its Proactive Commitment to the Security of General Aviation," H. Res. 120, U.S. Congress, House, 108th Cong., 1st sess., March 4, 2003, available online at http://frwebgate.access.gpo.gov/cgi-bin/get doc.cgi?dbname=108_cong_bills&docid=f:hr120ih.txt.pdf.

53. See http://www.aopa.org.

54. Aviation Security: Vulnerabilities and Potential Improvements for the Air Cargo System," GAO-03-344, U.S. General Accounting Office, December 2002, available online at http://www.gao.gov/new.items/d03344.pdf.

55. Hudson Morgan, "Shipping News," *New Republic*, July 7–14, 2003, p. 10.

56. Statement of Cathleen A. Berrick, "Aviation Security: Efforts to Measure Effectiveness."

57. Kay Bailey Hutchison, presiding officer, U.S. Congress, Senate, "Air Cargo Security Improvement Act" (S. 165), Proceedings and Debates of the 108th Cong., 1st sess., *Congressional Record*, May 8, 2003, p. S5932.

58. Morgan, "Shipping News."

59. "Security Risks in the Air," *Columbus Dispatch*, September 19, 2003, p. 14A.

60. For detailed history of the Aviation Security Advisory Committee, see E. Marla Felcher, "U.S. Aviation Security before and after the September 11

Terrorist Attacks," white paper, The Century Foundation, New York, February 2004, available online at http://www.tcf.org/Publications/Homeland Security/felcher_aviation.pdf.

61. "New Recommendations to Contribute to Improved Security in Air Cargo," press release, Transportation Security Administration, U.S. Department of Homeland Security, October 1, 2003, available online at http://www.tsa.gov/public/display?theme=44&content=0900051980059056.

62. Robert Kupperman, "Responses to Terrorism," hearing of the Governmental Affairs Committee, U.S. Congress, Senate, 101st Cong., 1st sess., Federal News Service, September 11, 1989.

63. The cause of the TWA explosion, while initially considered to be the work of terrorists, was ultimately ruled, five years after the crash, to be mechanical.

64. See http://www.opensecrets.org.

65. "TSA Screener Background Checks Fact Sheet," press release, Transportation Security Administration, U.S. Department of Homeland Security, September 29, 2003, available online at http://www.tsa.gov/public /display?theme=44&content=0900051980091914.

66. Brill, *After,* p. 30.

67. W. Kip Viscusi and Richard J. Zeckhauser, "Sacrificing Civil Liberties to Reduce Terrorism Risks," *Journal of Risk and Uncertainty* 26, nos. 2-3 (Special Issue on the Risks of Terrorism, March–May 2003): 99–120.

68. Statement of Kenneth M. Mead, inspector general, U.S. Department of Transportation, before the National Commission on Terrorist Attacks Upon the United States on Aviation Security, May 22, 2003, available online at http://www.oig.dot.gov/show_pdf.php?id=1101.

69. See the Web site of the Transportation Security Administration, U.S. Department of Homeland Security, http://www.tsa.gov.

CHAPTER 2

1. For a recommendation of a fleshed-out structure for sharing, one that resonates with many of the ideas in this paper, see *Creating a Trusted Network for Homeland Security: Second Report of the Markle Foundation Task Force,* Task Force on National Security in the Information Age, Markle Foundation, New York, December 2003, available online at http://www.markletaskforce.org/Report2_Full_Report.pdf. This quotation is from p. 8.

2. See, for instance, U.S. Congress, *Joint Inquiry into Intelligence Community Activities Before and After the Terrorist Attacks of September 11, 2001,* Report of the Senate Select Committee on Intelligence, and House Permanent Select Committee on Intelligence, 107th Cong., 2nd sess., December 2002, available online at http://a257.g.akamaitech.net/7/257/2422 /24jul20031400/www.gpoaccess.gov/serialset/creports/pdf/fullreport_errata.pdf.

3. Richard A. Clarke, *Against All Enemies: Inside America's War on Terror* (New York: Free Press, 2004).

4. *Creating a Trusted Network for Homeland Security,* p. 8.

5. "Fact Sheet: Strengthening Intelligence to Better Protect America," White House, January 28, 2003, available online at http://www.whitehouse.gov /news/releases/2003/01/20030128-12.html.

6. See "Warnings" page of the Web site for the Information Analysis and Infrastructure Protection Directorate, U.S. Department of Homeland Security, available online at http://www.nipc.gov/warnings/warnings.htm.

7. For a nice discussion of the differences, see Siobhan Gorman, "FBI, CIA Remain Worlds Apart," daily briefing, *Government Executive,* August 1, 2003, available online at http://www.govexec.com/dailyfed/0803 /080103nj1.htm.

8. See Gregory F. Treverton, *Reshaping National Intelligence for an Age of Information* (Cambridge: Cambridge University Press, 2001), p. 139ff.

9. The findings of the joint House-Senate investigation of September 11 outlines the basic story. See U.S. Congress, *Joint Inquiry into Intelligence Community Activities Before and After the Terrorist Attacks of September 11, 2001,* Part I of Final Report. A fuller account is contained in Senator Richard Shelby's supplementary document, "September 11 and the Imperative of Reform in the Intelligence Community: Additional Views of Senator Richard C. Shelby, Vice Chairman, Senate Select Committee on Intelligence," December 10, 2002, in particular, p. 15ff., available online at http://www.fas.org/irp/congress/2002_rpt/shelby.html.

10. See Gregory F. Treverton, "Intelligence, Law Enforcement, and Homeland Security," Homeland Security Project, The Century Foundation, New York, August 21, 2002, available online at http://www.homelandsec.org /Pub_category/pdf/treverton-intelligence.pdf. See also *Protecting America's Freedom in the Information Age: A Report of the Markle Foundation Task Force,* Task Force on National Security in the Information Age, Markle Foundation, New York, October 2002, available online at http://www.markletaskforce.org/documents/Markle_Full_Report.pdf.

11. For an analysis of the CTC and its role in homeland security see Stephen Marrin, "Homeland Security and the Analysis of Foreign

Intelligence," background research report prepared for *Protecting America's Freedom in the Information Age*, Task Force on National Security in the Information Age, Markle Foundation, New York, July 15, 2002, available online at http://www.markletaskforce.org/documents/marrin_071502.pdf.

12. "Fact Sheet: Strengthening Intelligence to Better Protect America," White House, February 14, 2003, available online at http://www.whitehouse.gov/news/releases/2003/02/20030214-1.html.

13. See Bruce Berkowitz, "A Fresh Start against Terror," *New York Times*, August 4, 2003, p. A13.

14. Including the CIA, FBI, Secret Service, Bureau of Alcohol, Tobacco, Firearms and Explosives (ATF), Immigration and Naturalization Service (INS), National Security Agency (NSA), State Diplomatic Security (SDS), Federal Aviation Administration (FAA), Naval Criminal Investigative Service (CIS), and Department of Energy (DOE).

15. *Homeland Security Act of 2002*, Public Law 107-296, *U.S. Statutes at Large* 116 (2002): 2135, Sec. 102.

16. For further details see "Campaign Financing Task Force: Problems and Disagreements Initially Hampered Justice's Investigation," Briefing Report to the Chairman, Committee on the Judiciary, U.S. Congress, House, GAO-GGD-00-101BR, U.S. General Accounting Office, May 31, 2000, available online at http://www.gao.gov/new.items/gg00101b.pdf.

17. See testimony of Robert S. Mueller III, director, Federal Bureau of Investigation, before the Senate Select Committee on Intelligence and the House Permanent Select Committee on Intelligence, U.S. Congress, Joint Intelligence Committee Inquiry, 107th Cong., 2nd sess., October 17, 2002, available online at http://www.fbi.gov/congress/congress02/mueller101702.htm.

18. For an interesting discussion of how other industrial democracies handle domestic intelligence and sharing among intelligence and law enforcement agencies, see Peter Chalk and William Rosenau, *Confronting the Enemy within: Security Intelligence, the Police, and Counterterrorism in Four Democracies* (Santa Monica, Calif.: RAND, 2004).

19. SCI is the broad category covering most intelligence information. But, as the name implies, that category is then broken down into compartments, for consumers, usually by source, with individual users then cleared into particular compartments. Some of those compartments, such as signal intelligence, or SIGINT, may have large numbers of people cleared into them; others are more specialized and smaller. But most FBI agents and almost all state and local law enforcement officers are *not* cleared into SCI at all.

20. Statement of David M. Walker, comptroller general of the United States, before the Subcommittee on Commerce, Justice, State and the

Judiciary, U.S. Congress, House, Committee on Appropriations, "FBI Reorganization: Initial Steps Encouraging but Broad Transformation Needed," GAO-02-865T, U.S. General Accounting Office, June 21, 2002, pp. 7–8, available online at http://www.gao.gov/new.items/d02865t.pdf; Fact Sheet: "Strengthening Intelligence to Better Protect America," February 14, 2003.

21. Conversations with the author.

22. For concerns that Trilogy won't perform as hoped, see Josh McHugh, "Rewiring the FBI: The FBI's $379 Million Upgrade Won't Solve the Agency's Problems," *Wired*, January 2002, available online at http://www.wired.com/wired/archive/10.01/mustread.html?pg=2.

23. As part of this effort, the FBI also has instituted a pilot Joint Terrorism Task Force Information Sharing Initiative (JTTF ISI) involving the St. Louis, San Diego, Seattle, Portland, Norfolk, and Baltimore field offices. This scheme is designed to incorporate flexible search tools that will permit investigators and analysts to perform full-text (as opposed to more narrow indexes) searches of investigative files.

24. "Homeland Security: Efforts to Improve Information Sharing Need to Be Strengthened," Report to the Secretary of Homeland Security, GAO-03-760, U.S. General Accounting Office, August 2003, pp. 9–10, available online at http://www.gao.gov/new.items/d03760.pdf.

25. The exceptions are mostly bigger states and cities. California, for instance, created an antiterrorism information center to share data within the state and with federal authorities. The New York Police Department has an intelligence office numbering several hundreds of officers. And New York, Pennsylvania, and Washington, D.C., have mounted, on their own initiative, a pilot project to share information in real time across the Internet. See "The Shield Pilot," available online at http://www.search.org/integration/pdf/ShieldPilot.pdf.

26. See "Homeland Security Presidential Directive/Hspd-6," White House, September 16, 2003, available online at http://www.whitehouse.gov/news/releases/2003/09/20030916-5.html.

27. "Information Technology: Terrorist Watch Lists Should Be Consolidated to Promote Better Integration and Sharing," GAO-03-322, U.S. General Accounting Office, April 15, 2003, available online at http://www.gao.gov/new.items/d03322.pdf.

28. *Foreign Intelligence and Surveillance Act, U.S. Code* 50 (1978), section 1804 (a) (7) (b), emphasis added.

29. Ibid., as amended by *USA Patriot Act of 2001,* Public Law 107-56, section 218, emphasis added.

30. See *Final Report of the Select Committee to Study Governmental Operations with Respect to Intelligence Activities,* U.S. Congress, Senate, 94th Cong., 2nd sess., April 14, 1976, Book II: Intelligence Activities and the Rights of Americans, and Book III: Supplementary Detailed Staff Reports on Intelligence Activities and the Rights of Americans. For links to these reports, as well as to a rich range of other documents, both historical and contemporary, see "Cointelpro," available online at http://www.icdc.com/~paulwolf/cointelpro/cointel.htm.

31. For background, see "FBI Pairs Criminal and Intelligence Cases," CNN.com, December 13, 2003, available online at http://www.cnn.com/2003/LAW/12/13/fbi.terrorism.ap/index.html.

32. Statement of David M. Walker, "FBI Reorganization," p. 12.

CHAPTER 3

1. U.S. Commission on Immigration Reform, *Becoming an American: Immigration and Immigrant Policy,* Report to Congress, September 1997, available online at http://www.utexas.edu/lbj/uscir/becoming/full-report.pdf.

2. One version, introduced after September 11, passed the House of Representatives in April 2002, several months before the administration announced its plans for a Department of Homeland Security. U.S. Congress, House, *Barbara Jordan Immigration Reform and Accountability Act of 2002,* HR 3231, 107th Cong., 2nd sess. (April 25, 2002).

3. Demetrios G. Papademetriou, T. Alexander Aleinikoff, and Deborah Waller Meyers, *Reorganizing the Immigration Function: Toward a New Framework for Accountability* (Washington, D.C.: Carnegie Endowment for International Peace, 1998).

4. See David A. Martin, "Immigration Policy and the Homeland Security Act Reorganization: An Early Agenda for Practical Improvements," *Insight* (Migration Policy Institute, Washington, D.C.), no. 1 (April 2003), available online at http://www.migrationpolicy.org/insight/insight_4-2003.pdf.

5. *Homeland Security Act of 2002,* Public Law 107-296, *U.S. Statutes at Large* 116 (2002): 2135, Section 445 (plan must detail how BTS will enforce the immigration laws "comprehensively, effectively and fairly"); Section 459 (requiring plan describing how USCIS will complete adjudications "efficiently, fairly, and within a reasonable time"). See also Section 478(b) (sense of Congress that after transfer of functions to DHS "quality and efficiency" of services should improve).

6. Ibid., Section 458 [amending Section 204(a)(1) of the *Immigration Services and Infrastructure Improvements Act, U.S. Code* 8 (2000), Section 1573(a)(1)].

7. The number of applications filed declined for each month after March 2003 until a spike in October 2003.

8. This was discovered when the FBI challenged an INS naturalization proceeding, asserting that the applicant was under surveillance by the bureau. The INS noted that the name had been run through the FBI database and had been cleared. The FBI then discovered that the name had not been checked against its other database.

9. The USCIS website registers about 3 million hits a month, and about 1 million forms are downloaded.

10. And 20 percent of 12 million calls a year means that the telephone system is generating 2.4 million dissatisfied customers for the agency.

11. *Homeland Security Act of 2002,* Section 452(a). Interestingly, the ombudsman is instructed to file reports directly with Congress without any prior comment from the USCIS director, the DHS secretary or deputy, or the OMB. *Homeland Security Act of 2002,* Section 452(c)(2). This arrangement raises difficult constitutional questions.

12. See the Web site of U.S. Immigration and Customs Enforcement, Department of Homeland Security, available online at http://www.ice.gov /graphics/about/index.htm.

13. "Memorandum to Regional Directors, District Directors, Chief Patrol Agents, Regional and District Counsel" from Doris Meissner, commissioner, Immigration and Naturalization Service, U.S. Department of Justice, November 17, 2000, available online at http://uscis.gov/graphics /lawsregs/handbook/discretion.pdf.

14. Interestingly, the prosecutorial discretion memorandum may be found on the USCIS Web site but not the ICE Web site.

15. This is not to say that all immigration-related policy is dominated by national security concerns, as is made clear in dramatic fashion by the recently unveiled Bush administration proposals on temporary workers.

16. Congress has mandated that all visa-waiver countries certify by October 26, 2004, that they are issuing machine-readable passports that incorporate biometric identifiers. It is unclear whether all covered countries will be able to meet this deadline and what impact a failure to do so will have on their nationals traveling to the Untied States after that date.

17. Both Richard Reid (born in the United Kingdom) and Zacarias Moussaoui (born in France) entered the United States under the visa-waiver program.

18. See David Martin's recommendation for a general counsel for immigration, reporting to the Department of Homeland Security's general counsel. Martin, "Immigration Policy and the Homeland Security Act Reorganization," p. 12. It might be advisable for the general counsel to appoint a deputy general counsel for immigration, refugees, and citizenship who could manage an intra-agency process and regulation writing on these topics.

19. The board was previously established by a regulation of the attorney general.

20. *Immigration and Nationality Act,* Section 103(a)(1), 8 U.S.C. §1103 (a)(1).

21. A process also must be put in place that establishes which department has the lead in drafting immigration-related regulations that have an impact both on DHS and the Exectuive Office for Immigration Review (examples might include detention, parole, and asylum regulations). David Martin has suggested that DHS have sole responsibility for drafting substantive regulations, with the Justice Department participating via the interagency review process run by OMB. See Martin, "Immigration Policy and the Homeland Security Act Reorganization," p. 21.

CHAPTER 4

1. "Initial National Response Plan," U.S. Department of Homeland Security, September 30, 2003, available online at http://www.dhs.gov/interweb /assetlibrary/Initial_NRP_100903.pdf.

2. See comments by Matthew Bettenhausen, director, Office for State and Local Government Coordination, U.S. Department of Homeland Security, in the transcript of the teleconference "Color-Coding Security: State Homeland Security Advisory Systems," Homeland Security Briefing Series, Council of State Governments, Lexington, Ky., July 9, 2003, text available online at http://www.csg.org/CSG/Policy/public+safety+and+justice/homeland+security /Transcript+-+July+9.htm; Eric Kelderman, "Law Enforcement Linking Tangled Information Webs," *Stateline.org* (Pew Center on the States, Pew Charitable Trusts, Washington, D.C.), December 9, 2003, available online at http://www.stateline.org/stateline/?pa=story&sa=showStoryInfo&id=338702.

3. Statement of Randall A. Yim, managing director, national preparedness, before the Subcommittee on Economic Development, Public Buildings, and Emergency Management, U.S. Congress, House, Committee on Transportation and Infrastructure, "National Preparedness: Integration of Federal, State,

Local, and Private Sector Efforts Is Critical to an Effective National Strategy for Homeland Security," GAO-02-621T, U.S. General Accounting Office, April 11, 2002, available online at http://www.gao.gov/new.items/d02621t.pdf.

4. Frank James, "Cities, States Fight Each Other for Homeland Security Dollars," Knight Ridder/Tribune News Service, April 7, 2003 p. K3991.

5. Interviewees for this report were assured they would not be identified by name and that their comments would not be linked to them.

6. Ruben Barrale, "Federalism in the Bush Administration," *Spectrum: The Journal of State Government* (Council of State Governments, Lexington, Ky.) 74, no. 3 (Summer 2001): 5.

7. "FY2004 Budget Fact Sheet," Office of the Press Secretary, U.S. Department of Homeland Security, October 1, 2003, available online at http://www.dhs.gov/dhspublic/display?content=1817.

8. Office of Management and Budget, Executive Office of the President of the United States, *Budget for Fiscal Year 2003* (Washington, D.C.: Government Printing Office, 2002), p. 937.

9. "Combating Terrorism: FEMA Continues to Make Progress in Coordinating Preparedness and Response," GAO-01-15, U.S. General Accounting Office, March 2001, available online at http://www.gao.gov /new.items/d0115.pdf; Statement of Arthur W. Cleaves, director, Maine Emergency Management Agency, before the Committee on Governmental Affairs, U.S. Congress, Senate, "Investing in Homeland Security: Challenges Facing State and Local Governments," 108th Cong., 1st sess., May 15, 2003, available online at http://govt-aff.senate.gov/_files/shrg10883hs_state local.pdf; Statement of Chauncey Bowers, on behalf of the International Association of Firefighters, before the Committee on Governmental Affairs, U.S. Congress, Senate, "Investing in Homeland Security: Challenges on the Frontline," 108th Cong., 1st sess., April 9, 2003, available online at http: //govt-aff.senate.gov/_files/040903bowers.pdf.

10. The two bills in question are the *Faster and Smarter Funding for First Responders Act of 2003*, HR 3266, 108th Cong., 1st sess., and the *Homeland Security Grant Enhancement Act of 2003*, S 1245, 108th Cong., 1st sess. Full text of the bills is available at http://thomas.loc.gov.

11. The grant programs primarily come from three separate entities: the Department of Justice, the Department of Health and Human Services, and FEMA (now the Directorate of Emergency Preparedness and Response). ODP was transferred to DHS from the Department of Justice.

12. "National Response Plan: Initial Plan: Draft," U.S. Department of Homeland Security, May 2003, available online at http://nemaweb.org/docs /National_Response_Plan.pdf.

13. Amy C. Hughes, "Summit Tackles Tough Issues: Emergency Response Organizations Meet to Discuss Key Issues for State and Local Government Preparedness," *State Government News* (Council of State Governments, Lexington, Ky.), August 2003, pp. 26–27, available online at http://www.ni2cie.org/SGN%20Article%20-%20Partnership%20Summit%20II.pdf.

14. "Comments on Draft National Response Plan," comments and letter e-mailed to the autor by Amy C. Hughes, policy analyst, National Emergency Management Association, Lexington, Ky., June 6, 2003; "Comments on Draft NRP Concept Plan," letter sent to Jeffrey Glick, supervisory program specialist, Emergency Preparedness and Response Directorate, U.S. Department of Homeland Security, from Ellen Gordon, response and recovery chair, National Emergency Management Association, Lexington, Ky., March 24, 2003; Amy C. Hughes, policy analyst, National Emergency Management Association, Lexington, Ky., e-mail correspondence with the author, November 20, 2003.

15. "Initial National Response Plan," p. 2.

16. Interview with the author, October 31, 2003.

17. Siobhan Gorman, "Homeland Security: Spreading the Faith," *National Journal*, October 10, 2003, available online at http://www.pscommllc.com/news/nj_hls_faith.html; Statement of Paul L. Posner, managing director, federal budget issues, strategic issues, before the Subcommittee on Government Efficiency, Financial Management, and Intergovernmental Relations, U.S. Congress, House, Committee on Government Reform, "Combating Terrorism: Intergovernmental Partnership in a National Strategy to Enhance State and Local Preparedness," GAO-02-547T, U.S. General Accounting Office, March 22, 2002, available online at http://www.gao.gov/new.items/d02547t.pdf.

18. Kate O'Beirne, "Introducing Pork-Barrel Homeland Security: A Little Here, A Lot There . . . ," *National Review*, August 11, 2003, available online at http://www.findarticles.com/cf_0/m1282/15_55/105891459/p1/article.jhtml.

19. Mimi Hall, "Homeland Security Money Doesn't Match Terror Threat: Does Zanesville, Ohio, Need to Test for Nerve Agents as NYC Struggles for Funds?" *USA Today*, October 29, 2003, p. 1A, available online at http://www.usatoday.com/news/washington/2003-10-29-security-cover-usat_x.htm.

20. Ibid.

21. Eric Kelderman, "Panel Urges Anti-Terrorism Spending Guidelines," *Stateline.org* (Pew Center on the States, Pew Charitable Trusts, Washington, D.C.), December 15, 2003, available online at http://www.stateline.org/stateline/?pa=story&sa=showStoryInfo&id=339674.

22. James, "Cities, States Fight Each Other for Homeland Security Dollars."

23. "Federal Homeland Security Assistance to America's Hometowns: A Survey and Report from the Democratic Task Force on Homeland Security," U.S. Congress, October 29, 2003, available online at http://www .house.gov/maloney/issues/Homeland/Survey.pdf. However, see "State Spending of Homeland Security Funds," report by the National Emergency Management Association, Lexington, Ky., April 2, 2003, available online at http://nemaweb.org/Library/Documents/State_Administration_of_Homeland _Security_Funds.pdf, for an alternative perspective on the transfer of money from states to local governments.

24. *Forging America's New Normalcy: Securing Our Homeland, Protecting Our Liberty,* Fifth Annual Report to the President and Congress of the Advisory Panel to Assess Domestic Response Capabilities for Terrorism Involving Weapons of Mass Destruction (Gilmore Commission), December 15, 2003, Appendix D, p. D-2-3, Table 2A, available online at http://www.rand.org/nsrd/terrpanel/volume_v/volume_v_appendices_only.pdf.

25. Marcos Mocine-McQueen, "Funding Scarce for Homeland Security in Colorado: State Department Lags as No Money Set Aside," *Denver Post,* December 17, 2003, p. A29.

26. International Association of Firefighters, Washington, D.C., letter to Christopher Cox, chairman, and Jim Turner, ranking member, Select Committee on Homeland Security, U.S. Congress, House of Representatives, November 19, 2003, available online at http://www.hsc.house.gov/files /InternationalAssnOfFFightersEndorsement.pdf; Statement of Philip C. Stittleburg, chairman, National Volunteer Fire Council, Washington, D.C., on HR 3266, n.d., available online at http://www.hsc.house.gov/files /NatVolFireCouncilEndorsement.pdf.

27. Alice Lipowicz, "Bad Omen? As Federal Grants Reach the States Squabbling Begins," *CQ Homeland Security,* CQ.com, Congressional Quarterly Inc., Washington, D.C., December 3, 2003.

28. Paul Magnusson, "America's Cities Are Seeing Red over Code Orange," *Business Week*, June 9, 2003, p. 55, available online at http: //www.businessweek.com/magazine/content/03_23/c3836069_mz013.htm; "U.S. Conference of Mayors Announces: 90 Percent of Cities Left Empty-Handed without Funds from Largest Federal Homeland Security Program," press release, United States Conference of Mayors, Washington, D.C., September 17, 2003, available online at http://www.usmayors.org/uscm /news/press_releases/documents/homelandfunding_091703.pdf.

29. Mocine-McQueen, "Funding Scarce for Homeland Security in Colorado."

30. *Emergency Responders: Drastically Underfunded, Dangerously Unprepared,* report of an independent task force sponsored by the Council on Foreign Relations, New York, June 2003, Executive Summary, p. 1, available online at http://www.cfr.org/pdf/Responders_TF.pdf.

31. Cited in statement of Chauncey Bowers, "Investing in Homeland Security."

32. Christopher Cox, "Intelligence for First Responders," *Washington Times,* September 10, 2003, p. A19, available online at http://hsc.house.gov /coverage.cfm?id=77.

33. Statement of Paul L. Posner, managing director, federal budget issues and intergovernmental relations, strategic issues, before the Subcommittee on Terrorism, Technology and Homeland Security, U.S. Congress, Senate, Committee on the Judiciary, "Homeland Security: Reforming Federal Grants to Better Meet Outstanding Needs," GAO-03-1146T, U.S. General Accounting Office, September 3, 2003, available online at http://www .gao.gov/new.items/d031146t.pdf.

34. Statement of Jeffrey Horvath, chief of police, Dover, Delaware, before the Committee on Governmental Affairs, U.S. Congress, Senate, "Investing in Homeland Security: Challenges on the Front Line," 108th Cong., 1st sess., April 9, 2003, available online at http://govt-aff.senate.gov/index.cfm ?Fuseaction=Hearings.Testimony&HearingID=82&WitnessID=294.

35. Statement of Robert F. Dacey, director, information security issues, before the Subcommittee on Cybersecurity, Science, and Research and Development and the Subcommittee on Infrastructure and Border Security, U.S. Congress, House, Select Committee on Homeland Security, "Homeland Security: Information Sharing Responsibilities, Challenges, and Key Management Issues," GAO-03-1165T, U.S. General Accounting Office, September 17, 2003, available online at http://www.gao.gov/new.items /d031165t.pdf; Statement of William O. Jenkins, Jr., director, homeland security and justice issues, before the subcommittees of the Government Reform Committee, U.S. Congress, House, "Homeland Security: Challenges in Achieving Interoperable Communications for First Responders," GAO-04-231T, U.S. General Accounting Office, November 6, 2003, available online at http://www.gao.gov/new.items/d04231t.pdf.

36. Glen Woodbury, director, Emergency Management Division, Military Department, Washington State, "TOPOFF 2: Washington State Agencies' Lessons Learned," presentation at the National Emergency Management Association annual conference, Seattle, September 9, 2003.

37. Cited by Robert Block, "FEMA Points to Flaws, Flubs in Terror Drill," *Wall Street Journal,* October 31, 2003, B1.

38. Jim Mullen, director, Division of Emergency Management, City of Seattle, "Lessons Learned from the Seattle TOPOFF Exercise," *IAEM Bulletin* (International Association of Emergency Managers, Falls Church, Va.) 20, no. 7 (July 2003): 10.

39. Block, "FEMA Points to Flaws, Flubs in Terror Drill"; Woodbury, "TOPOFF 2."

40. A public version of the report was released by the Department of Homeland Security on December 19, 2003, "Top Officials (TOPOFF) Exercise Series: TOPOFF 2—After Action Summary Report for Public Release," available online at http://www.dhs.gov/interweb/assetlibrary/T2_Report_Final _Public.doc. While the public report points out challenges associated with the Homeland Security Alert System and other issues, a more critical evalua-tion of the exercise is revealed by accounts of participants presented at a National Emergency Management Association conference, as well as an internal review of the exercise conducted by FEMA and reported on by Robert Block in the WSJ. See, for example, Eric Holdeman, director, Office of Emergency Management, King County, Washington, "TOPOFF2 Exercise Design: Washington Venue," presentation at the National Emergency Management Association annual conference, September 9, 2003.

41. Donald F. Kettl, "The States and Homeland Security: Building the Missing Link," report, Working Group on Federalism Challenges, Homeland Security Project, The Century Foundation, New York, 2003, available online at http://www.tcf.org/Publications/HomelandSecurity/kettl.pdf.

42. Louise K. Comfort, "Assessment of Homeland Security Initiatives: Commonwealth of Pennsylvania," report, Working Group on Federalism Challenges, Homeland Security Project, The Century Foundation, New York, 2003, p. 30–32, available online at http://www.tcf.org/Publications /HomelandSecurity/comfort.pdf.

43. Dennis L. Dresang, "Strengthening Federal-State Relationships to Prevent and Respond to Terrorism," report, Working Group on Federalism Challenges, Homeland Security Project, The Century Foundation, New York, 2003, p. 20, available online at http://www.tcf.org/Publications/Homeland Security/dresang.pdf.

44. Steven D. Stehr, "Homeland Security in the State of Washington: A Baseline Report on the Activities of State and Local Governments," report, Working Group on Federalism Challenges, Homeland Security Project, The Century Foundation, New York, 2003, p. 27, available online at http: //www.tcf.org/Publications/HomelandSecurity/stehr.pdf.

45. Kelderman, "Panel Urges Anti-Terrorism Spending Guidelines."

46. *National Strategy for Homeland Security*, Office of Homeland Security, White House, July 2002, p. vii, available online at http://www .whitehouse.gov/homeland/book/nat_strat_hls.pdf.

47. Ben Canada, "Homeland Security: Standards for State and Local Preparedness," Report for Congress, Congressional Research Service, Library of Congress, updated October 8, 2003, pp. 24–25.

48. Alice Lipowicz, "Fire Chiefs Smoldering over Low Seat at the Homeland Table," *CQ Homeland Security, Local Response,* CQ.com, Congressional Quarterly Inc., Washington, D.C., August 13, 2003, available online at http://www.acs.ohio-state.edu/homelandsecurity/focusareas /emergencyprep.html.

49. Ibid.

50. Alan Caldwell, "FIRE Act Grants for FY '04 Funded at $750 Million; Moved to ODP," *IAFC On Scene* (International Association of Fire Chiefs, Fairfax, Va.) 17, no. 18 (October 15, 2003): 1, 6, available online at http://www.iafc.org/data/fullissue/Oct1503.pdf.

51. Keith Bea, "Proposed Transfer of FEMA to the Department of Homeland Security," Report for Congress, Congressional Research Service, Library of Congress, July 29, 2002, p. 7–21, available online at http://www .usembassy.at/en/download/pdf/homelandsec_fema.pdf.

52. *Coping with Catastrophe: Building an Emergency Management System to Meet People's Needs in Natural and Manmade Disasters* (Washington, D.C.: National Academy of Public Administration, 1993); Saundra K. Schneider, *Flirting with Disaster: Public Management in Crisis Situations* (Armonk, N.Y.: M. E. Sharpe, 1995).

53. Walter Pincus, "FEMA's Influence May Be Cut under New Department," *Washington Post,* July 24, 2002, p. A17, available online at http: //www.washingtonpost.com/ac2/wp-dyn/A53075-2002Jul23?language=printer.

54. "Comments on Draft National Response Plan."

55. "Initial National Response Plan," p. 1.

56. *Homeland Security Act of 2002,* Public Law 107-296, 116 *U.S. Statutes at Large* 2135, Sec. 507.

57. Office of Management and Budget, *Budget for Fiscal Year 2003,* pp. 933–38; "President Announces Substantial Increases in Homeland Security Budget," press release, Office of the Press Secretary, White House, January 24, 2002, available online at http://www.whitehouse.gov/news/releases/2002 /01/20020124-1.html.

58. The important Emergency Management Performance Grants are still allocated through FEMA. The fiscal year 2004 budget also places responsibility

for several public health initiatives, including the Metropolitan Medical Response Program, with FEMA, as well as grants for planning and preparation of major metropolitan health systems for disasters and cash stockpiles for emergency pharmaceuticals and training of public health personnel. "FY2004 Budget Fact Sheet," Office of the Press Secretary, Department of Homeland Security, October 1, 2003, available online at http://www.dhs .gov/dhspublic/display?content=1817.

59. *Homeland Security Act of 2002*, Sec. 430.

60. A link to DHS.gov is identified in small print at the bottom of the FEMA home page next to the privacy policy, accessibility, how to find FEMA in Spanish, and the site index. See the Web site of the Federal Emergency Management Agency, available online at http://www.FEMA.gov.

61. See the Web site of the Office for Domestic Preparedness, U.S. Department of Homeland Security, available online at http://www.ojp.usdoj .gov/odp/.

62. *A Governor's Guide to Emergency Management, Volume Two: Homeland Security*, NGA Center for Best Practices, National Governors Association, Washington, D.C., 2002, p. 12, available online at http://www.nga.org/cda/files/GOVSGUIDEHS2.pdf.

63. Kettl, "States and Homeland Security"; Statement of Paul L. Posner, "Combating Terrorism."

64. Interview with the author, November 7, 2003.

65. Andrew Mitchell, deputy director, Office for Domestic Preparedness, Department of Homeland Security, "Office for Domestic Preparedness: Overview Briefing," presentation at the National Emergency Management Association annual conference, Seattle, September 8, 2003.

66. "States Struggle to Pay for Homeland Security," Associated Press, January 28, 2003, available online at http://www.foxnews.com/story /0,2933,76829,00.html.

67. Mocine-McQueen, "Funding Scarce for Homeland Security in Colorado."

68. The link is https://justice.ojp.usdoj.gov/dct, State Homeland Security Assessment and Strategy Program, Office for Domestic Preparedness, U.S. Department of Homeland Security, available only to "pre-designated Government agencies" and specified contractors.

69. Ibid.

70. Hughes, "Summit Tackles Tough Issues."

71. *After-Action Report on the Response to the September 11 Terrorist Attack on the Pentagon*, Arlington County, Virginia, n.d., available online at http://www.co.arlington.va.us/fire/edu/about/pdf/after_report.pdf.

72. For example, three bureaus (operations, special operations, and wellness, safety, and training) support the Division of Fire and Rescue Services of Montgomery County, Maryland. See http://www.montgomerycountymd.gov /mcgtmpl.asp?url=/mc/services/dfrs/dfrs.asp. Similarly four divisions support the Arlington County (Virginia) Fire Department: administration services, technical services, operations and emergency services, and fire prevention and community services. See http://www.co.arlington.va.us /fire/edu/about/dept_org.htm#.

73. *Homeland Security Act of 2002*, Sec. 882.

74. The Metropolitan Washington Council of Governments Web address is http://www.mwcog.org/home.asp. A similar use of the COG system is in place in Texas. See Robie Robinson, David A. McEntire, and Richard T. Weber, "Texas Homeland Defense Preparedness," report, Working Group on Federalism Challenges, Homeland Security Project, The Century Foundation, New York, 2003, available online at http://www.tcf.org/Publications /HomelandSecurity/robinson.pdf. See also the Web site of the Mid-America Regional Council (MARC), which serves the bistate Kansas City region in a similar manner, available online at http://www.marc.org/.

75. See "HR3266, Faster and Smarter Funding for First Responders: A Comprehensive Summary," on the Web site of the Select Committee on Homeland Security, U.S. Congress, House, available online at http://homeland .house.gov.

76. See the *Homeland Security Grant Enhancement Act of 2003*, especially Sec. 3.

INDEX

Note: Page numbers followed by letters *f, n,* and *t* refer to figures, notes, and tables, respectively.

Accenture, 36

Aguirre, Eduardo, 80, 82

Air cargo: percentage transported on passenger planes, 9, 44; security gaps in, 8–9, 11, 30, 44–45; security recommendations for, 12

Air marshal service: expansion of, 8, 11, 30, 40–41, 47; as innermost layer of protection, 32

Aircraft Operators and Pilots Association, 43

Airlines: donations to political campaigns, 46–47, 124*n*51; passenger information collected by, sharing with TSA, 39–40; resistance to aviation security, 46, 50; responsibility for aviation security, 31

Airport checkpoint screeners: Aviation and Transportation Security Act mandate for, 32; background checks for, 8, 10–11, 33–34, 47; effectiveness of, 34; hiring of, 7–8, 10, 29–30, 33, 36, 47; improvements in, 47; performance data on, need for,

34–35; questions about, 30; before September 11, 2001, 31; training and testing of, 34, 47

All-hazards approach, 106–7; and domestic security, relationship between, 109–10; FEMA and, 107, 108–9; need to maintain, 108; vs. terrorism-specific preparedness, 107–8, 109

Attorney general, and immigration law and policy, 93–94

Aviation and Transportation Security Act (ATSA), 29; on airport perimeters and access controls, 41; goals set by, 31, 32; shortcomings of, 48, 50

Aviation security, 29–51; assessment of improvements in, 34–35; DHS performance with respect to, 3, 4, 10–11; media tests of, 35; new vulnerabilities in, 42; progress in, 29–30, 37–41, 47–48; recommendations for, 12; remaining gaps in, 8, 11, 30, 35, 42–45; as ring of protective layers, 31–32; before

September 11, 2001, 31, 45–47; shortage of money for, 37, 38, 42; trade-offs connected to, 48–51; vulnerability revealed on September 11, 2001, 2, 10; as work in progress, 50; zero-risk mentality and, 49. *See also* Transportation Security Administration (TSA)
Aviation Security Advisory Committee, 45

Baggage. *See* Air cargo; Luggage
Berrick, Cathleen A., 40
Bettenhausen, Matthew, 131*n*2
Bishop, Charles J., 43
Board of Immigration Appeals, 91, 93
Boeing, and aviation security, 36
Border and Transportation Safety Directorate, 78, 79; accomplishments of, 90; and USCIS, coordination between, 92–93
Border Patrol: expansion under Clinton administration, 78; transfer to DHS, 79
Bureau of Citizenship and Immigration Services (USCIS), 78; backlog in application processing, 80–83; and Border and Transportation Safety Directorate, coordination between, 92–93; customer service at, 83–84; and ICE, coordination between, 91, 92; and National Security Entry-Exit Registration

System, 82; ombudsman's office within, 83–84, 130*n*11; Web site of, 130*n*9
Bureau of Customs and Border Protection, 79; agents at, 85
Bureau of Immigration and Customs Enforcement (ICE): agents at, 85; and air marshal service, 41; and FBI, competition between, 88; mission of, 85–86; new toughness in, 87; operations of, 86; reorientation of priorities at, 87–88; and USCIS, coordination between, 91, 92
Bush, George H. W., on aviation security, 46
Bush, George W.: and Aviation and Transportation Security Act, 29; and DHS, creation of, 1, 13; on Immigration and Naturalization Service (INS), 78; on immigration backlog, 79; immigration reform proposal of (2004), 80, 130*n*15; and Magaw (John) appointment, 31, 33, 52

Caldwell, Alan, 108
California: antiterrorism information center in, 128*n*25; homeland security funding for, 18, 102
CAPPS II. *See* Computer-Assisted Passenger Prescreening System
Central Intelligence Agency (CIA): Counterterrorism Center of, 56*t*, 66, 67; data provided to

IAIP, 61; and FBI, 13, 63, 65, 67, 69, 71; independence from DHS, 13, 55; President's Daily Brief of, 67, 68
Civil liberties, concerns over, 74; passenger profiling and, 38–39; watch lists and, 72–73
Clarke, Richard, 59
Clinton, Bill, on aviation security, 46
"Code Orange" security alerts, cost of, 103
COINTELPRO, 73–74
Cold war, intelligence dichotomies during, 63–64, 74
College of Analytical Studies, 68
Computer-Assisted Passenger Prescreening System (CAPPS II), 30, 38–40, 47
Computer systems, need for improvements in, 24
Congress: on air cargo security gap, 44–45; ambivalence on security-commerce dichotomy, 50; and aviation security, goals for, 32–33, 34, 36; and DHS, problems in relationship of, 9–10; and DHS grant distribution, approaches to, 113–16, 114t–115t; on general aviation security gap, 43; and grants to state and local governments, 102; and money for aviation security, 37, 38, 42, 46
Coordination: need for, 24; problems with, 7, 14, 104–6; recommendations for, 18–19
Counterterrorism Center (CTC), 56t, 66, 67

Counterterrorism Division (CTD), FBI, 56t, 66, 69–70
Cox, Christopher, 104
Customs and Border Protection. See Bureau of Customs and Border Protection
Customs Service: data provided to IAIP, 61; integration into DHS, 78, 85

Dacey, Robert F., 135n35
Defense Intelligence Agency, Joint Task Force for Combating Terrorism, 67
Delaware, first responders in, challenges facing, 104
DEP. See Directorate for Emergency Preparedness
Department of Defense (DOD), creation of, 1
Department of Energy, data provided to IAIP, 61
Department of Homeland Security (DHS): accomplishments of, 7–8; campaign for creation of, 13, 55; efficiency of, 41; and information analysis, capacity for, 67–68; and information gathering, capacity for, 58, 62; and information sharing, task of, 71; location of, 20; management of, 3, 6, 20–24; mission of, 1–2, 21–22; organization of, 26f–27f; organizational "tiger team" in, proposal for, 23–24; overlapping roles with other agencies, 13, 55; personnel of, 1, 20; prevention vs. response in strategy of, 22; report card for, 3–7;

risk in creating, 20; scale and complexity of, 1, 20; shortcomings of, 8–10, 117. *See also specific agencies and fields of work*

Department of Justice: Board of Immigration Appeals at, 91, 93; Executive Office for Immigration Review at, 93

DHS. *See* Department of Homeland Security

Directorate for Border and Transportation Safety. *See* Border and Transportation Safety Directorate

Directorate for Emergency Preparedness (DEP): and all-hazards approach, 107; and ODP, relationship between, 19; responsibilities of, 19, 99*t*, 109

Downey, Mortimer, 22

Drug Enforcement Administration, data provided to IAIP, 61

Eisenhower, Dwight D., 50

Elson, Steve, 35

Explosives detection systems: Aviation and Transportation Security Act on, 32; Boeing contract for, 36; and improved aviation security, 38, 47; integration into baggage-handling systems, 37–38

Federal air marshals. *See* Air marshal service

Federal Aviation Act (1958), 50

Federal Aviation Administration (FAA): assistance to TSA, 36; creation of, 50; "no-fly" list of, 47–48; responsibilities of, 31; spending on aviation security, 48; stalling of security regulations at, 45

Federal Bureau of Investigation (FBI): change in mission of, 57, 62; and CIA, 13, 63, 65, 67, 69, 71; and COINTELPRO, 73–74; Counterterrorism Division of, 56*t*, 66, 69–70; data provided to IAIP, 61; and ICE, competition between, 88; and immigration screening, 81, 130*n*8; independence from DHS, 13, 55; internal audits, findings of, 68; and joint terrorism task forces, 71, 128*n*23; mission prior to September 11, 2001, 59; National Capital Response Squad of, 112; Office of Intelligence of, 56*t*, 68; organizational culture of, 62, 69; reorganization at, 68, 69–70, 74; technology upgrade at, 70; upgrading of intelligence in, 68

Federal Emergency Management Agency (FEMA), 100; and all-hazards approach, 107, 108–9; grants allocated through, 137*n*58; transformation in 1990s, 108. *See also* Directorate for Emergency Preparedness

Federal Protective Service, functions taken over by DHS, 78

Feinstein, Dianne, 44

FEMA. *See* Federal Emergency
  Management Agency
Firefighters: grant programs for,
  100; at homeland security
  task force meetings, 108
First responders: all-hazards
  approach and, 107–8; DHS
  focus on, 58; federal aid to,
  allocation problems, 18, 98,
  102–3; preparedness gap
  among, 103–4; on September
  11, 2001, 17
FISA. *See* Foreign Intelligence and
  Surveillance Act
Foreign Intelligence and
  Surveillance Act (FISA), eas-
  ing restrictions of, 73, 74

General aviation (private planes),
  42; security gaps in, 8, 11,
  30, 42–43; security recommendations for, 12
Gilmore Commission report, 18,
  102–3
Glauthier, T. J., 22
Grants, DHS: allocation problems,
  18, 98, 102, 103; application
  process, complexity of, 104;
  congressional approaches to
  distribution of, 113–16,
  114*t*–115*t*; disbursement
  problems, 102–3; Office of
  Domestic Preparedness
  (ODP) and, 98, 100, 104; uti-
  lization questions, 102

Homeland Security Act, 79
Homeland Security Alert System,
  98; problems with, 105
Hoover, J. Edgar, 64

Horvath, Jeffrey, 104, 136*n*34
House Select Committee on
  Homeland Security, 116;
  approach to DHS grant dis-
  tribution, 113, 114*t*–115*t*
Hughes, Patrick, 58
Hutchinson, Asa, 86, 87, 91; on
  US-VISIT, 89
Hutchison, Kay Bailey, 44

IAIP. *See* Information Analysis
  and Infrastructure Protection
  Directorate
ICE. *See* Bureau of Immigration
  and Customs Enforcement
Immigration, 77–95; appeals, 91,
  93; Attorney general's role,
  93–94; backlog in application
  processing, 9, 80–83; border
  enforcement, 88–91; coordination problems, 9, 80–83,
  91–93; customer service,
  83–84; DHS functions related
  to, 78–79, 96*f*; DHS performance with respect to, 3, 5,
  15–16, 80–91; division of
  enforcement and service functions, 84, 87, 94; interior
  enforcement, 85–88; recommendations for, 16–17, 94–95;
  registration programs, 86–87;
  security checks in, 81, 130*n*8;
  vulnerability revealed on
  September 11, 2001, 2, 15, 78
Immigration and Customs
  Enforcement (ICE). *See*
  Bureau of Immigration and
  Customs Enforcement
Immigration and Naturalization
  Service (INS): abolition of,

79; problems of, 15, 77–78; restructuring of, results from, 7; transfer to DHS, 78, 84–85

In-Q-Tel, 72

Indiana, homeland security challenges in, 106

Information analysis, 65–68; DHS capacity for, 67–68; TTIC and, 65–67

Information Analysis and Infrastructure Protection (IAIP) Directorate, 8, 17, 57–58, 60–62; briefings published by, 61–62; data analyzed by, 61; role of, 61, 62; and Terrorist Threat Integration Center (TTIC), 57, 61, 66; threat assessment by, 60

Information gathering, 73–74; DHS capacity for, 58, 62; recommendations for, 65; by state and local authorities, 73

Information sharing, 69–73; Border and Transportation Safety Directorate and, 90; gaps in, 58–59, 69; lack of infrastructure for, 72; progress in, 69–73; recommendations for, 65; with state and local governments, 14, 58, 60, 65, 71–72; TTIC and, 60, 66, 71

Information sharing and analysis centers (ISACs), 62

Initial National Response Plan (2003), 97–98, 101, 108

INS. *See* Immigration and Naturalization Service

Intelligence, domestic, 55–75. *See also* Information analysis; Information gathering; Information sharing; agencies involved in, 56*t*; challenges to, 57; coordination problems, 7, 14; current status of, 57; deficiencies in, 58–59; DHS capacity for, 58, 62, 67–68; DHS performance with respect to, 3, 4, 13–14, 55, 57–59; FBI and, 68; vs. foreign intelligence, 63–64; IAIP and, 60–62; innovations in, 59; vs. law enforcement, 63, 69; progress in, 57–58; public vs. private, 64; recommendations for, 14–15, 65; roots of failure before September 11, 2001, 63–65; TTIC and, 65–67; vulnerability revealed on September 11, 2001, 2, 13, 58–59

Intelligence analysts, sources of, 62

ISACs. *See* Information sharing and analysis centers

Jackson, Michael, 31

Jenkins, William O., Jr., 136*n*35

JetBlueAirways, 39

Joint terrorism task forces, 71, 128*n*23

Jordan Commission (1997), 77

King, Martin Luther, Jr., 74

Kinney, Joseph A., 43

Kupperman, Robert, 45–46

Law enforcement, vs. intelligence, 63, 69

Liberty: and security, balance between, 74. *See also* Civil liberties, concerns over

Local governments. *See* State and local governments

Lockheed Martin, 36

Louie, Gilman, 72

Loy, James, 33, 41, 45, 52, 54

Luggage: in air cargo, security gaps for, 8–9; checked, screening of, 30, 32, 37–38, 47

Magaw, John: appointment as TSA chief, 31, 52; problems experienced by, 32–33

Management of DHS: recommendations for, 21–24; report card for, 3, 6, 20–21

Markey, Edward J., 45

Markle Foundation task force, 17–18, 58, 60, 72

Martin, David, 131n18, 131n21

McHale, Steven, 35

Mead, Kenneth, 50

Media, tests of airport security, 35

Meissner, Doris, 87

Metropolitan Washington Council of Governments, 112, 139n74

Michigan, homeland security spending in, 103

Mineta, Norman, 31, 33

Mitigation, 107

Money: for aviation security, 37, 38, 42; "Code Orange" security alerts and, 103; for state and local governments, 18, 98, 102–4. *See also* Grants

Moussaoui, Zacarias, 73, 130n17

Mueller, Robert, 68, 69

Mullen, Jim, 136n38

National Capital Region Emergency Preparedness Council, 112

National Commission on Terrorist Attacks Upon the United States, 2, 50

National Infrastructure Protection Center, 57, 61

National Joint Terrorism Task Force, 70–71

National Security Agency: data provided to IAIP, 61; independence from DHS, 13, 55

National Security Entry-Exit Registration System (NSEERS), 82, 86–87; effectiveness of, 94

NCS Pearson, 36–37

New York: antiterrorism information sharing in, 128n25; homeland security funding for, 18, 102

North Dakota, homeland security funding for, 102

NORTHCOM, 67

Northwest Airlines, 40

NSEERS. *See* National Security Entry-Exit Registration System

Oberstar, James L., 43, 124n51

Office of Domestic Preparedness (ODP): Assistance to Firefighters, 108; and DEP, relationship between, 19; and domestic security preparedness, funding for, 109; grant programs of, 98, 100, 104;

responsibilities of, 19, 99*t*;
State Homeland Security
Strategies required by,
110–11
Office of Information Analysis,
role of, 56*t*
Office of Intelligence, FBI, 56*t*, 68
Office for National Capital Region
Coordination, 99*t*, 112
Office for State and Local
Government Coordination
(OSLGC), 99*t*, 100
Ornstein, Norman J., 21

Pan Am Flight 103 bombing, 45,
46
Passenger profiling, 30, 38–40,
47–48; public criticism of,
38–39
Pennsylvania: antiterrorism infor-
mation sharing in, 128*n*25;
homeland security challenges
in, 106
Posner, Paul L., 135*n*33
Preparedness, 107
President's Daily Brief, 67, 68
President's Terrorism Threat
Report, 57, 67; Office of
Intelligence and, 68
Privacy concerns, passenger profil-
ing and, 38–39
Private planes. *See* General aviation

Railroads, warning systems of, 62
Redmond, Paul, 58, 62
Reid, Richard, 130*n*17
Response and recovery, 107
Ridge, Tom, 100; challenges for,
20, 21; deputy secretary of,
23

Rogers, Harold, 32–33
Rowley, Coleen, 13

SA-7 shoulder-fired missiles, 42
Schumer, Charles E., 34
Security: and liberty, balance
between, 74. *See also*
Aviation security
Senate Governmental Affairs
Committee, approach to
DHS grant distribution,
113–14, 114*t*–115*t*
September 11, 2001: aviation
security prior to, 31, 45–47;
first responders on, 17; and
immigration processing backlog, 81–82; and impetus for
change, 69; roots of failure
in, 63–65; vulnerabilities
revealed by, 1–2, 10, 13, 15,
58–59, 78; warnings about,
59
SEVIS. *See* Student and Exchange
Visitor Information System
Southern Poverty Law Center, 62
State and local governments: challenges for improvement in
relations between, 106–16;
DHS offices working with,
99*t*; DHS performance with
respect to, 3, 6, 17–18,
97–101; DHS requirements
from, 110–11; federal aid to,
allocation problems, 9,
18–19, 98, 102–4; information gathering by, 73; information sharing with, 14, 58,
60, 65, 71–72, 98; Initial
National Response Plan
(2003) and, 97–98, 101;

model for building strategic partnership with, 111–12; needs of, 110; problems in coordination with, 104–6; recommendations for coordination with, 18–19; vulnerability revealed on September 11, 2001, 2

State Homeland Security Strategy, 110–11

Stone, David M., 40, 54

Student and Exchange Visitor Information System (SEVIS), 86

Students, foreign, tracking entry and matriculation of, 7, 16, 86

Technology: impediments to information sharing, 72; improved, need for, 24, 70

Tenet, George, 68

Terrorism: campaign against, impact on private citizens, 64; nature of threat, 24; targeting, vs. all-hazards approach, 107–8, 109. *See also* September 11, 2001

Terrorist Identity Data Mark, 72

Terrorist Screening Center, 17, 72

Terrorist Threat Integration Center (TTIC), 13, 55, 57, 65–67; concerns about, 67; and information analysis, 65–67; and Information Analysis and Infrastructure Protection (IAIP) Directorate, 57, 61, 66; and information sharing, 60, 66, 71; mandate of, 66; obstacles to work of,

66–67; overlapping responsibilities within, 14; and President's Terrorism Threat Report, 57, 67; role of, 56*t*; and Terrorist Identity Data Mark, 72

Threat assessment, vs. vulnerability assessment, 60

"TIPOFF" watch lists, 72

TOPOFF exercise (2003), 19, 105, 136*n*40

Trace detection machines, 37, 47

Transportation Department, data provided to IAIP, 61

Transportation Security Administration (TSA), 29–45; accomplishments of, 29–30, 37–41; and air cargo security, 44–45; and air marshal service, 8, 11, 30, 40–41; and airport checkpoint screeners, 7–8, 10–11, 29–30, 33–34; and airport perimeters and access controls, 41–42; budget of, 29, 31; contractors hired by, 36; creation of, 29; deadlines imposed by Congress on, 32, 33, 36; first leader of, 31, 32–33; first year of, 49; functions taken over by DHS, 78; and general aviation security, 43; history of, timeline of significant events, 52*t*–54*t*; mandate of, 32; mission statement of, 50–51; and passenger profiling, 30, 38–40; questions before, 49; reorganization of, 7–8; second year of, 49; shortcomings of, 30,

42–45; spending by, 36–37, 48; third year of, 49
Transportation Workers Identification Card (TWIC), 30, 41
Trilogy, 70
Truman, Harry, 64
TSA. *See* Transportation Security Administration
TTIC. *See* Terrorist Threat Integration Center
TWA 747 explosion, 46, 125*n*63
TWIC. *See* Transportation Workers Identification Card

Unisys, 41
Urban Areas Security Initiative grant programs, 100
US-VISIT, 88–91; effectiveness of, 94; gaps in, 91
USA Patriot Act (2001), 73
USCIS. *See* Bureau of Citizenship and Immigration Services

VF Solutions, 36
Virginia, strategic planning in, 111
Visa-waiver program, 88, 89, 130*n*16–17

Viscusi, Kip, 49

Washington, D.C.: antiterrorism information sharing in, 128*n*25; model for building strategic partnership with state and local governments, 111–12
Washington State, homeland security challenges in, 106
Watch lists: and civil liberties questions, 72–73; consolidation and sharing of, need for, 65, 72
Web sites, 109, 130*n*9
Wisconsin, homeland security challenges in, 106
Witt, James Lee, 108
Woodbury, Glen, 135*n*36
Wyoming, homeland security funding for, 18, 102

Yim, Randall A., 131*n*3
Young, Don, 44

Zeckhauser, Richard, 49
Zero-risk mentality, 49
Ziglar, James, 82

ABOUT THE CONTRIBUTORS

T. ALEXANDER ALEINIKOFF is executive vice president for law and dean of the Law Center at Georgetown University, where he has been a professor since 1997. He is also a senior associate at the Migration Policy Institute. He served in two positions at the Immigration and Naturalization Service during the Clinton administration, first as general counsel and then as executive associate commissioner for programs. He is the author of *Semblances of Sovereignty: The Constitution, the State, and American Citizenship* (Harvard University Press, 2002); coauthor, with David A. Martin and Hiroshi Motomura, of *Immigration and Citizenship: Process and Policy* (Foundation Press, 2003); and coeditor, with Vincent Chetail, of *Migration and International Legal Norms* (T. M. C. Asser Press, 2003).

E. MARLA FELCHER is a freelance journalist and adjunct lecturer of public policy at Harvard University's Kennedy School of Government. She has worked in marketing for Gillette and the Talbots and as a market research consultant for Ben & Jerry's, J. Crew, Monro Muffler & Brake, and Nabisco. She has written about the regulation of consumer products for *Mother Jones*, the *Atlantic Monthly*, *Child*, *Wildlife Conservation*, and the Understanding Government project (www.understandinggovt.org). She is the author of *It's No Accident: How Corporations Sell Dangerous Baby Products* (Common Courage Press, 2001).

DONALD F. KETTL is Stanley I. Sheerr Endowed Term Professor in the Social Sciences at the University of Pennsylvania, where he teaches in the Department of Political Science and the Fels Institute of Government. He previously served as a faculty member at the

University of Wisconsin-Madison, Vanderbilt University, the University of Virginia, and Columbia University. He is the author of, among other books, *System under Stress: Homeland Security and American Politics* (CQ Press, 2004) and *The Transformation of Governance: Public Administration for Twenty-First Century America* (John Hopkins University Press, 2002); and coauthor, with James W. Fesler, of *The Politics of the Administrative Process,* 3rd edition (Seven Bridges Press, 2002).

ANNE M. KHADEMIAN is an associate professor with the Center of Public Administration and Policy in the School of Public and International Affairs at Virginia Tech. She taught political science and public affairs at the University of Wisconsin-Madison, held visiting positions at the University of Michigan and the University of Pennsylvania, and was a research fellow at the Brookings Institution. Her books include *Working with Culture: How the Job Gets Done in Public Programs* (CQ Press, 2002); *Checking on Banks: Autonomy and Accountability in Three Federal Agencies* (Brookings Institution Press, 1996); and *The SEC and Capital Market Regulation: The Politics of Expertise* (University of Pittsburgh Press, 1992).

GREGORY F. TREVERTON is a senior policy analyst at RAND, where he formerly directed the International Security and Defense Policy Center and is currently associate dean for research of the Pardee RAND Graduate School. His recent work has examined terrorism, intelligence, and law enforcement, with a special interest in new forms of public-private partnership. He has served in government for the first Senate Select Committee on Intelligence, for the National Security Council handling European affairs, and for the National Intelligence Council as vice chair, overseeing the writing of America's National Intelligence Estimates (NIEs). His most recent book is *Reshaping National Intelligence for an Age of Information* (Cambridge University Press, 2001).